Memoirs of the Life and Writings of Lindley Murray

by Lindley Murray

Address:
HardPress
8345 NW 66TH ST #2561
MIAMI FL 33166-2626
USA
Email: info@hardpress.net

Memoirs of the life and writings of Lindley Murray

Lindley Murray, Elizabeth Frank

182

Emily Wilkinson.

in remembrance of the

Authoress.

…lethorpe Hall.

…istmas

1858

Westoby pinxit — *sculpsit*

Lindley Murray

Publd by Longman & Co London and Wilson & Sons York.

Septr 14 1826

MEMOIRS

OF

THE LIFE AND WRITINGS

OF

LINDLEY MURRAY:

IN A SERIES OF LETTERS,

WRITTEN BY HIMSELF.

WITH A PREFACE, AND

A CONTINUATION OF THE MEMOIRS,

BY ELIZABETH FRANK.

SECOND EDITION.

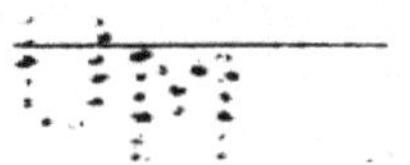

York:

Printed by Thomas Wilson and Sons, High-Ousegate:

PUBLISHED BY LONGMAN, REES, ORME, BROWN, AND GREEN;

AND HARVEY AND DARTON, LONDON: AND

WILSON AND SONS, YORK.

1827.

PREFACE.

In presenting this little volume to the public, I am solicitous to state the reasons which led to its publication; and I flatter myself they will prove satisfactory.

The celebrity which the subject of these Memoirs had obtained, and the interest which he had excited, by his arduous and successful endeavours to promote the literary, moral, and religious improvement of youth, often induced me to think that, after his decease, a short and authentic account of his life and character, would be acceptable to the public. To that part of the public more immediately benefited by his labours, the work would, I apprehended, prove peculiarly pleasing.

Under these impressions, I made, at different periods, some notes and observations, preparatory to an undertaking of this nature. I was, however, sensible that, from various circumstances, particularly from my not having been acquainted with Mr. Murray till he was considerably advanced in life, I was not qualified to execute the task as I could wish. I was convinced too, that no person, except himself, possessed that accurate knowledge of the events of his life, and the formation of his character, which would render the work truly interesting and instructive. His friends in America had had but little intercourse with him, except by letter, since the fortieth year of his age: his friends in England had, of course, known him only since that period, when his character and principles were formed; and from the ill state of his health, his subsequent life was spent in retirement. I had heard various reports respecting him, and I had also seen a printed account, which, though apparently not originating in any ill will, or in any ill design, were utterly void of foundation. * I was apprehensive, that, after

* I do not, by any means, allude to a short biographical sketch, inserted in the European Magazine, 1803; and thence

his death, some of these accounts, or others of a similar nature, might obtain currency, and even find their way into respectable publications, if not prevented by a true and well authenticated statement of facts.

These circumstances induced me earnestly to wish that he might become his own biographer. But I knew that the delicacy of his mind would, at least in the first instance, revolt at the proposal. I therefore contented myself with hinting to him my intention of writing, if I should survive him, a short account of his life; and I requested his assistance only in supplying me with a few materials, relative to the period preceding my acquaintance with him. It was not without many arguments, and much solicitation, that I could induce him to acknowledge the propriety of my proposal, and to promise compliance. The work, however, was not begun till long afterwards; and it was frequently suspended,

---

copied into various periodical publications: that account, as far as it goes, is perfectly authentic; and, in every particular, strictly consistent with the tenour of these Memoirs.

on account of his numerous literary avocations, and the weak state of his health. At length, after many interruptions, and demurs respecting its propriety, it was completed, in a series of letters addressed to myself. I was so well pleased with the performance; and I believed that it would be so much more agreeable and interesting in the author's own words and manner, than in any I could devise; that I relinquished my original idea. I could not be satisfied to receive what he had written, as materials only: but I strongly urged him to continue the work to the time of his writing; and to allow me, (if circumstances should seem to require the measure,) to publish it, after his decease, in the form in which he had written it. To this, after much consideration, he consented; continuing to express an apprehension, that neither the subject, nor the manner in which it is treated, is worthy of public notice and approbation: an opinion in which, I believe, few readers will concur.

As some persons may be inclined to think, that I acted improperly in inducing him to write these Memoirs, and afterwards to consent to their publication, I must, in justice to myself, be allowed to make a few observations on the subject. Many pious persons have written memoirs of their own lives, and some even purposely for publication; and such works have been perused with much interest and edification by the most respectable part of the community. I should not have urged the proposal, had I not been persuaded that Mr. Murray's objections to it, had no other foundation than a humble sense of his own merit, and an unwillingness to intrude himself unnecessarily on the attention of the world; and that the removing of these objections, might, without doing him any injury, or exciting any improper sentiments in his mind, be the means of introducing to the public a pleasing and instructive little work. Without his consent, I should not have deemed myself authorized to publish it; fully concurring in sentiment with him, that the publishing of any letter, without permission from the writer, is, to say the least, a flagrant breach of decorum, of honour, and of that confidence which is the basis of all social and friendly intercourse.

If, notwithstanding this explanation, there should still, in the apprehension of any person, appear the slightest cause of censure, I trust that it will fall on the editor who first suggested the idea of the work, and strongly urged the execution of it; and not, in any degree, on the departed author. I can truly say, that every sentiment which he expressed, during the whole course of the discussion, was strictly consistent, on the one hand, with the integrity of his principles, and the delicacy of his feelings; and on the other, with the wish which he candidly avowed, of not unnecessarily withholding any thing, that might tend to the gratification of friendship, and of innocent or even laudable curiosity, if not to the promotion of higher objects.—The suggestion that the serious reflections with which this little work abounds, might be beneficial, especially to young persons, seemed much to reconcile him to the publication.

It may not be improper to state, that these Memoirs are published exactly as I received them from the author: I have neither added, nor diminished, any thing; not having thought myself at liberty, nor indeed having any wish, to make the slightest variation.

I have annexed to the Memoirs, a short account of the concluding years of the author's life, his character, and some remarks on his various publications: an addition that seemed necessary to complete the information, which this little volume is designed to convey. In what I have written, I am not sensible that I have, in any respect, departed from the exact truth. I can, on this occasion, fully adopt the sentiment which Dr. Beattie expresses with regard to his son: "In order to convey a favourable notion of the person of whom I speak, I have nothing to do but to tell the simple truth."

I had abundant opportunity of being acquainted with the life and character of the late much esteemed Lindley Murray.—During many years, from motives of friendship to himself and his wife, I lived under his roof; and afterwards, having removed into a house, which I had purchased in the suburbs of the city of York, about half a mile from his residence, I was in the habit of visiting them very frequently. Some readers may, indeed, think that I have given unnecessary proof of intimate acquaintance, by relating many particulars, which they may deem too minute. To them it may appear that I have, with an unhallowed or injudicious hand, removed the veil, which retirement had cast over my friend, and which shaded him from the glare of public observation. But it must be allowed, that in the representation which I have given of him, I have only exhibited him to the many as he appeared to the comparatively few, who were intimately acquainted with him; and that the more he was known, the more he was loved and esteemed. In his character there was no affected singularity; and in his habits there were no peculiarities, except such as resulted from a judicious or necessary conformity to unavoidable circumstances. Nor was there any thing in his conduct, or even in the detail of his domestic arrangements, which required concealment; or which could not bear the test of near approach, and close examination. I may further shield myself under the example and authority of Dr. Johnson. In his Lives of the Poets, he narrates, with evident satisfaction, and I am sure most persons will peruse with interest, many particulars apparently more trivial than any which I have related: and in his Rambler, he judiciously observes; "The business of the biographer is to lead the thoughts into domestic privacies, and display the minute details of daily life."

I should with much pleasure, agreeably to my own wish, and to the suggestion of others, have enriched this work with a selection from Mr. Murray's letters, or with copious extracts from them: but I am not authorized to assume this privilege. On a particular occasion he received an application for leave to publish some of his letters; which, after mature deliberation, he declined giving. The subject was thus brought under his consideration; and in consequence he expressed, very strongly, both at that time and subsequently, his wish and request that after his decease, none of his letters should on any occasion, or in any manner, be published. And that his request might not be forgotten, nor his meaning misunderstood, he has left it in writing. He never, I am convinced, wrote a line of which he had cause to be ashamed: but his letters, though multifarious, were chiefly on subjects of private or family business, or on his literary concerns; or effusions written on the spur of the moment, relating to incidents or occasions of a local and temporary nature.—In objecting to the publication of his letters, he was influenced, not merely by modesty, but by various considerations.

Some years since, the proprietors of his works, with great liberality, requested him to allow them to have his portrait taken by an eminent artist; which I am sorry to say, he declined. Several little sketches were made, by various persons who occasionally visited him: but all of these had little if any resemblance of him, except a profile, which I have received through the kindness of Mr. Sansom of Philadelphia. It was taken by him, in 1799, when he was on a visit at Holdgate; but it has not yet been engraven.—After Mr. Murray's decease, several persons went to view his remains: amongst others, Mr. Westoby, a miniature painter, who for his own satisfaction, made a sketch of the features of the deceased; from which he afterwards formed the portrait which is now annexed to this volume.

It is scarcely necessary to observe that, if any profit should arise to the editor, from the publication of Mr. Murray's Memoirs, it will, in conformity with his practice, be applied, like that on all his other works, to charitable and benevolent purposes.

I present to the public the Memoirs which my friend has written of his life, with a firm, but humble confidence, that they will meet a favourable reception; and that few readers will find any thing to regret in them but their brevity. They will perhaps not be unacceptable or uninteresting, as a correct and pleasing specimen of the epistolary style, and as the last composition that will be produced to the world, of an esteemed and highly useful writer: for with respect to the few manuscripts which he has left, none are prepared, or designed, for publication; and in regard to his letters, his request will, I doubt not, be held sacred. But this little volume possesses stronger and more important claims to favour and approbation than any I have yet mentioned. To the philosopher, it affords a striking instance of a character formed to a high degree of excellence, and rising into eminence, not by adventitious advantages, but chiefly by its own native energy and exertion; to the moralist, the virtuous principles which it recommends, and which, in some degree, it exemplifies from the earliest dawn of reason to the latest period of life, will doubtless be highly gratifying; to the young, it will, I trust, prove a stimulus to the due improvement of their intellectual and moral powers, and the dedication of them to the glory of their great Creator, and the benefit of their fellow-creatures: and on all, it will, I hope, forcibly inculcate the important lesson of pious acquiescence in the Divine Will, and the duty and happiness of cultivating, even under trying and discouraging circumstances, a contented, cheerful, and benevolent disposition.

The Mount, York,
August, 1826.

MEMOIRS.

MEMOIRS,

&c.

LETTER I.

My dear Friend,

I HAVE not forgotten the repeated and urgent requests which have been made to me, to communicate some memoirs of my life, especially of its earlier periods, for the gratification of friendship. But a reluctance to write so particularly on the subject of myself, and my own concerns, has hitherto prevented me from engaging in a work of this nature. I cannot, however, any longer refuse to comply with a proposal, which is supported by the soothing recommendations of esteem and regard, and by a friendship which has subsisted between us for many years. But after all, I am doubtful whether any parts of such a life as mine has been, can afford much satisfaction, or answer the expectations which may have been formed on the subject. Perhaps, indeed, when I shall have bidden adieu to this transient scene, the events here recorded, may acquire an interest, which, at present, they do not possess. If this should be the case, and they should sometimes excite the recollection of our friendship, and produce reflections of a pleasing or useful nature, they will not have been wholly written in vain. With these views then, I enter on my little history. And as it will have some advantages, I shall form the narrative into a series of familiar letters.

It is always a delicate point to speak, or to write, properly, concerning one's self. But as I have been persuaded to undertake a work involving this difficulty, I must accommodate myself to it, as well as I am able. Being at once the subject and the narrator, it will not be possible to prevent a very frequent recurrence of the obnoxious pronoun. I will, however, study so to conduct this biographical sketch, as to avoid every species of undue self prominence, as well as to repress whatever may be considered as false delicacy. If I should sometimes err, in prosecuting these intentions, I have no doubt the veil of indulgence and friendship will be thrown over my imperfections.

I was born in the year 1745, at Swetara, near Lancaster, in the state of Pennsylvania. My parents were of respectable characters, and in the middle station of life. My father possessed a good flour mill at Swetara: but being of an enterprising spirit, and anxious to provide handsomely for his family, he made several voyages to the West Indies, in the way of trade, by which he considerably augmented his property. Pursuing his inclinations, he, in time, acquired large possessions, and became one of the most respectable merchants in America.

In the pursuit of business, he was steady and indefatigable. During the middle period of his life, he had extensive concerns in ships; and was engaged in a variety of other mercantile affairs. But this great and multifarious employment, never appeared to agitate or oppress his mind: he was distinguished for equanimity and composure. And I have often heard it remarked, that, by his conversation and deportment, no person would have imagined, that he had such a weight of care upon him. When in the company of his friends, he was so thoroughly unbent, that persons unacquainted with the nature and variety of his business, might naturally suppose that he had very little employment. This trait may be justly considered as an evidence of strong powers of mind. These had been cultivated by attention to business, and by much intercourse with the world. But my father did not possess the advantages of a liberal education; by which his talents and virtues might have been still more extensively useful.

My mother was a woman of an amiable disposition, and remarkable for mildness, humanity, and liberality of sentiment. She was, indeed, a faithful and affectionate wife, a tender mother, and a kind mistress. I recollect, with emotions of affection and gratitude, her unwearied solicitude for my health and happiness. This excellent mother died some years after I had been settled in life. And though I had cause to mourn for the loss of her, yet I had reason to be thankful to Divine Providence, that I had been blessed with her for so long a period, and particularly through the dangerous seasons of childhood and youth.

Both my parents, who belonged to the society of Friends, were concerned to promote the religious welfare of their children. They often gave us salutary admonition, and trained us up to attend the public worship of God. The Holy Scriptures were read in the family: a duty which, when regularly and devoutly performed, must be fraught with the most beneficial effects. I recollect being, at one time, in a situation of the room, where I observed that my father, on reading these inspired volumes to us, was so much affected as to shed tears. This, which I suppose was frequently the case, made a pleasing and profitable impression on my young mind, which I have often remembered with peculiar satisfaction.—Our family was rather numerous. My parents had twelve children, of whom I was the eldest. But the course of time has reduced us to a small number. At the present period, (the summer of 1806,) only four of us remain.

That activity of body, for which I was remarkable in youth and mature life, commenced at an early age.* When I was only nine months old, I frequently escaped, as I have been informed, from the care of the family: and, un-

* The first months of the author's life afforded no promise either of bodily or mental vigour. Till he was about half a year old, he was almost perpetually crying. His countenance gave no indication of intelligence. His mother was little aware of the comfort which she should afterwards receive from him, and of the honourable distinction which awaited him. She often said, that if, at that time, Providence had been pleased to take away her first-born, she should have thought the dispensation merciful, both to the poor little infant and its parents. But after that period, his health gradually improved; and his strength, spirit, and activity, exceeded his age. From various accounts, and from many little anecdotes, which I have heard, I cannot but conclude, that his childhood and youth were lovely; and formed a natural and beautiful prelude to the wisdom, piety, and benevolence, which his advanced years exhibited. Though from his extraordinary vivacity, and exuberance of spirits,

noticed by them, made my way from the house to the mill, which were more than a hundred yards distant from each other. As soon as I could run about, I proved to be, not only an active, but a mischievous child. I played many tricks, which did not denote the best disposition, and which gave a wrong bias to my vivacity. This perverse turn of mind might have been checked in the bud, if it had received suitable, early correction.

But I had a very fond grandmother, with whom I was a great favourite, and who often protected me from proper chastisement, when I richly deserved it. This indulgence gave full scope to my propensities; and prevented, for a time, that happy restraint, which is of so much importance to the disposition and habits of children, and which has so much influence on their happiness through life. The irregular vivacity which I possessed, received, however, a very salutary control, by my being afterwards placed under the care of a discreet and sensible aunt,

---

he was inclined to playfulness, and frolic, and, at times, to some degree of mischievousness; yet he possessed every quality that can adorn that period of life: activity of body and mind; an ardent desire for knowledge; docility in submitting to superior reason; a mild, obliging temper; a heart, grateful, affectionate, and highly susceptible of religious feelings.

EDITOR.

who was determined to bring me into some degree of order and submission. The great indulgence with which I had been treated, must have rendered the contest rather severe: for, on a particular occasion, I embraced the opportunity of getting out of a window, and running about on the roof of a small tenement; which was, however, so high, that a fall would have endangered my life. My aunt was in great distress; and I believe endeavoured, but in vain, to influence my fears, and, by this means, induce me to return. I moved about for a while, in this perilous situation, and probably enjoyed my temporary independence. She, at last, with great prudence, entreated me very tenderly to come to her. But though this affected me, I did not comply till I had obtained her promise, that I should not be corrected. She kept her word; but I think she did not relax, in any degree, the general rigour of her discipline towards me. I was at length completely subdued, and brought into regular obedience: and this event proved comfortable to myself, as well as relieving to every one that had any care of me. To this good aunt I am under particular obligations. Her wise and salutary management, may have prepared me for many enjoyments, and prevented many miseries of life.

At an early period, about my sixth or seventh year, I was sent to the city of Philadelphia, that I might have the advantage of a better school than the country afforded. I well remember being some time at the academy of Philadelphia ; the English department of which was then conducted by the truly respectable Ebenezer Kinnersley. He exercised great care over his pupils : and from what I recollect of this instructer of youth, and what I have read of him, I have reason to regret, that my continuance in that seminary was of short duration. I remember to have read there with pleasure, even at that age, some passages in " The Travels of Cyrus ;" and to have been agreeably exercised in the business of parsing sentences.

From this academy I was taken, to accompany my parents to North Carolina. My father conceived, that some commercial advantages would attend a temporary residence in that province. When I first landed there, I was much delighted with roving about, after a long confinement on ship board. In one of these little excursions, I found a few shillings ; which were readily expended in some loaves of bread, for the refreshment of the sailors. These people had been kind to me, during the voyage ; and I could not, therefore, think of any more pleasing application of my treasure, than in treating them with some excellent fresh bread. Their grateful acceptance, and enjoyment, of this little gift, was doubtless a rich reward for my attention to them.

In the year 1753, my father left Carolina; and, with his family, settled at New York. In this city, I was placed at a good school, in which I made the usual progress of young learners. Being extremely fond of play, I believe I rarely neglected any opportunity of indulging this propensity. At the times of vacation, I generally enjoyed myself with diversions, till the period for returning to school approached. I then applied myself vigorously to the task that had been previously assigned me; and I do not recollect that I ever failed to perform it, to the satisfaction of my teacher. A heedless boy, I was far from reflecting, how much more prudent it would have been, if I had, in the first place, secured the lesson, and afterwards indulged myself in my playful pursuits. These would not then have been interrupted, by uneasy reflections on the subject of my task, or by a consciousness of unwarrantable negligence.—Sometimes I absented myself from school, to enjoy a greater degree of play and amusement. During these pleasures, the idea of impending correction, would occasionally come across my mind: but I resolutely repelled it, as an intruder which would unnecessarily imbitter my present enjoyment. I concluded that if I must be corrected, I would not lose the pleasure I then had; and I gave full scope to my diversions. Had I allowed myself proper time to consider consequences, I might have prevented both the disgrace and the pain of punishment, as well as that degree of insensibility to dishonourable action, which such fearless irregularities are apt to produce.

About this period, a very happy impression was made on my mind, by a piece which was given me to write, and in the performance of which I had to exhibit a specimen of my best hand writing. The sheet was decorated round its edges with a number of pleasing figures, displayed with taste and simplicity. In the centre, my performance was to be contained. This was a transcript of the visit and salutation of the angels to the shepherds, near Bethlehem, who were tending their flocks by night. The beauty of the sheet; the property I was to have in it; and the distinction which I expected from performing the work in a handsome manner; prepared my mind for relishing the solemn narrative, and the interesting language of the angels to the shepherds. I was highly pleased with the whole. The impression was so strong and delightful, that it has often occurred to me, through life, with great satisfaction; and, at this hour, it is remembered with pleasure. The passage has scarcely ever been read by me, without emotions of an interesting nature. Independently of the attractive circumstances which I have depicted, the narrative and message are, indeed, most important and affecting to every serious mind.—If parents and others who have the care of young persons, would be studious to seize occasions of presenting the Holy Scriptures to them, under favourable and inviting points of view, it would probably be attended with the happiest effects. A veneration for these sacred volumes, and a pleasure in perusing them, may be excited by agreeable and interesting associations; and these impressions, thus early made, there is reason to believe, would accompany the mind through the whole of life: a consideration which is of the utmost importance.

But though I might sometimes be disposed, at this period of life, to think and to act properly, I was often impelled by inclinations of a very different nature. I had a curious propensity to discover and observe the natural dispositions of animals. And this curiosity was, in some instances, so strong as to make me overlook the uneasiness which, by teasing them, was occasioned to the animals themselves. I was not naturally of a cruel disposition; but was rather pleased to see the animal creation about me, enjoy themselves. The propensity I have mentioned was, however, sometimes unwarrantably indulged: so much so, as to mark a depraved turn of mind, which, even now, gives me pain to recollect.—I ought to have reflected, that all animals have assigned to them by the Author of nature, a pleasurable existence; and that it is our duty to second his intention, as we have opportunity; and especially to avoid all occasions of inflicting upon them unnecessary pain. An additional excitement to this duty, is, that whilst we encourage a disposition to promote the pleasures, or increase the pains, of the animals which surround us, we are cherishing the general spirit of benevolence, or its contrary; which will naturally be extended towards our fellow-creatures. In this point of view, it is of very great importance to cultivate, in young persons especially, proper dispositions and conduct towards the creatures endued with animal life.

The unwarrantable curiosity which I have just mentioned, continued to operate, in some degree, for many years; and, occasionally, showed itself long after I was grown up. I recollect a particular instance of it, which was very near proving fatal to me; and which, though a little out of the course of my narrative, may not improperly be related in this place. As nearly as I can recollect, the incident was as follows.

When I was in England, in the year 1771, I went to see the elephants, which were kept at the Queen's stables, Buckingham-house. Whilst I was gratifying myself with observing the huge creatures, and their various actions and peculiarities, I took occasion to withdraw from one of them a part of the hay, which he was collecting on the floor with his proboscis. I did this with my cane; and watched the animal very narrowly, to prevent a stroke from him, which I had reason to expect. The keeper said that I had greatly displeased the elephant, and that he would never forget the injury. I thought but little of this admonition, at the time. But about six weeks afterwards, when I accompanied some other persons, on a visit to the elephants, I found that, though probably several hundred people had been there since my preceding visit, the animal soon recognised me. I did not attempt to molest or tease him at all; and I had no conception of any concealed resentment. On a sudden, however, when I was supposed to be within the reach of his proboscis, he threw it towards me with such violence, that if it had struck me, I should probably have been killed, or have received some material injury. Happily for me, I perceived his intention, and being very active, I sprung out of his reach. To every other person present, he was gentle and good-tempered; and

his enmity to me arose, as the keeper declared, solely from the circumstance of the little affront which I had formerly put upon him.—This incident made some impression upon me; and perhaps contributed to subdue a curiosity, which could not be gratified but at the expense of the feelings of others.

It is now time to make a pause in the narrative. My next letter will pursue it, from the period of my leaving school, and being trained to business.

I am affectionately, &c.

LETTER II.

My dear Friend,

It is doubtless of great importance to the interest and happiness of young persons, as well as of some consequence to their friends and the public, that their inclinations, genius, and bodily constitutions, should be consulted, when they are to be entered on an employment, which will probably continue for life. If the bent of their mind, and other qualifications, are duly regarded, success may reasonably be expected: if they are opposed, the progress must be slow, and the ultimate attainments very limited.

At an early age, I was placed in the counting house of my father, who was desirous of training me to the mercantile profession. I did not, however, relish this employ, and the confinement to which it subjected me. I wished to be any thing rather than a merchant. And this, perhaps, may be accounted for, by the strictness with which I was kept to business, and the undue restraints, as I conceived, which were put, at that early period, on my lively spirits and allowable indulgences. My father kept steady to his purpose. He probably thought that my dislike to the business would, in time, abate. He sent me to Philadelphia, influenced, perhaps, by a hope, that a residence with a merchant at a distance from home, would better reconcile me to the employment. But this expedient did not answer his expectation ; and after some time, he consented to my return to New York.

About this period, I contracted a taste for reading, and a desire for a greater degree of literary improvement. The pleasures of study, and the advantages and distinctions, which learning and knowledge had conferred on individuals who fell under my observation, augmented my wishes for the acquisition of science and literature.—Another experiment was, however, made to reconcile me to a mercantile life. My father presented me with a considerable number of silver watches, which he designed as a little trading stock ; and which he had just imported, with many other articles, from England. By having the property of these watches, and by the prospect of increasing that property on the sale of them, and thus extending my concerns, in fresh purchases with the product, I began to relish the occupation. The spirit of trading took hold of me ; and I contemplated, with pleasure, the future enlargement of my funds. In short, I entered into the business with ardour and satisfaction. At the same time I continued in my father's counting house; and occasionally assisted in the routine of his commercial affairs.—I doubt not, that he surveyed this success of his schemes for my advantage, with peculiar complacency. But not long after the commencement of my trading engagements, an incident occurred, which seemed to blast all his expectations, and to threaten the most serious consequences to myself.

I have sometimes hesitated, respecting the propriety of communicating this little piece of my history. But as it is intimately connected with events of this period, and contains some traits of disposition and character in early life, I have at length concluded to relinquish my scruples on this subject. The following is the occurrence to which I allude.

Though my father, as the events already mentioned demonstrate, had an earnest desire to promote my interest and happiness, yet he appeared to me, in some respects, and on some occasions, rather too rigorous. Among other regulations, he had, with true parental prudence, given me general directions not to leave the house, in an evening, without previously obtaining his approbation. I believe that his permission was generally and readily procured. But a particular instance occurred, in which, on account of his absence, I could not apply to him. I was invited by an uncle to spend the evening with him; and trusting to this circumstance, and to the respectability of my company, I ventured to break the letter, though I thought not the spirit, of the injunction which had been laid upon me. The next morning, I was taken by my father, into a private apartment, and remonstrated with for my disobedience. In vain were my apologies. Nothing that I could offer, was considered as an extenuation of my having broken a plain and positive command. In short, I received a very severe chastisement; and was threatened with a repetition of it, for every similar offence. Being a lad of some spirit, I felt very indignant at such treatment, under circumstances which, as I conceived, admitted of so much alleviation. I could not bear it; and I resolved to leave my father's house, and seek, in a distant country, what I conceived to be an asylum, or a better fortune. Young and ardent, I did not want confidence in my own powers; and I presumed that, with health and strength which I possessed in a superior degree, I could support myself, and make my way happily through life. I meditated on my plan; and came to the resolution of taking my books and all my property with me, to a town in the interior of the country; where I had understood there was an excellent seminary, kept by a man of distinguished talents and learning. Here I purposed to remain, till I had learned the French language, which I thought would be of great use to me; and till I had acquired as much other improvement as my funds would admit. With this stock of knowledge, I presumed that I should set out in life under much greater advantages, than I should possess by entering immediately into business, with my small portion of property, and great inexperience. I was then about fourteen years of age. My views being thus arranged, I procured a new suit of clothes, entirely different from those which I had been accustomed to wear, packed up my little all, and left the city, without exciting any suspicion of my design, till it was too late to prevent its accomplishment.

In a short time, I arrived at the place of destination. I settled myself immediately as a boarder in the seminary, and commenced my studies. The prospect which I entertained was so luminous and cheering, that, on the whole, I did not regret the part I had acted. Past recollections and future hopes combined to animate me. The chief uneasiness which I felt in my present situation, must have arisen from the reflection of having lost the society and attentions of a most affectionate mother, and of having occasioned sorrow to her feeling mind. But as I had passed the Rubicon, and believed I could not be comfortable at home, I contented myself with the thought, that the pursuit of the objects before me, was better calculated than any other, to produce my happiness. In this quiet retreat, I had as much enjoyment as my circumstances were adapted to convey. The pleasure of study, and the glow of a fond imagination, brightened the scenes around me. And the consciousness of a state of freedom and independence, undoubtedly contributed to augment my gratifications, and to animate my youthful heart. But my continuance in this delightful situation, was not of long duration. Circumstances of an apparently trivial nature, concurred to overturn the visionary fabric I had formed, and to bring me again to the paternal roof.

I had a particular friend, a youth about my own age, who resided at Philadelphia. I wished to pay him a short visit, and then resume my studies. We met according to appointment, at an inn on the road. I enjoyed his society, and communicated to him my situation and views. But before I returned to my retreat, an occurrence took place which occasioned me to go to Philadelphia. When I was about to leave that city, as I passed through one of the streets, I met a gentleman who had some time before dined at my father's house. He expressed great pleasure on seeing me; and inquired when I expected to leave the city. I told him I was then on the point of setting off. He thought the occasion very fortunate for him. He had just been with a letter to the postoffice; but found that he was too late. The letter, he said, was of importance; and he begged that I would deliver it with my own hand, and as soon as I arrived at New York, to the person for whom it was directed. Surprised by the request, and unwilling to state to him my situation, I engaged to take good care of the letter.

My new residence was at Burlington, about twenty miles from Philadelphia. I travelled towards it rather pensive, and uncertain what plan to adopt respecting the letter. I believe that I sometimes thought of putting it into the postoffice; sometimes, of hiring a person to deliver it. But the confidence which had been reposed in me; the importance of the trust; and my tacit engagement to deliver it personally; operated so powerfully on my mind, that after I had rode a few miles, I determined, whatever risk and expense I might incur, to hire a carriage for the purpose, to go to New York as speedily as possible, deliver the letter, and return immediately. My design, so far as it respected the charge of the letter, was completely accomplished. I delivered it, according to the direction, and my own engagement. I was, however, obliged to remain in New York that night, as the packet boat, in which I had crossed the bay, could not sail till the next morning. This was a mortifying circumstance, as I wished to return very expeditiously. The delay was, however, unavoidable. I put up at an inn, near the wharf from which the packet was to sail in the morning, and waited for that period with some anxiety.

I thought I had conducted my business with so much caution, that no one acquainted with me, had known of my being in the city. I had, however, been noticed by some person who knew me; and, in the evening, to my great surprise, my uncle, whom I have mentioned before, paid me a visit. He treated me affectionately, and with much prudent attention; and, after some time, strenuously urged me to go with him to my father's house: but I firmly refused to comply with his request. At length he told me, that my mother was greatly distressed on account of my absence; and that I should be unkind and undutiful, if I did not see her. This made a strong impression upon me. I resolved, therefore, to spend a short time with her, and then return to my lodgings. The meeting which I had with my dear and tender parent was truly affecting to me. Every thing that passed, evinced the great affection she had for me, and the sorrow into which my departure from home had plunged her. After I had been some time in the house, my father unexpectedly came in: and my embarrassment, under these circumstances, may easily be conceived. It was, however, instantly removed, by his approaching me in the most affectionate manner. He saluted me very tenderly; and expressed great satisfaction on seeing me again. Every degree of resentment was immediately dissipated. I felt myself happy, in perceiving the pleasure which my society could afford to persons so intimately connected with me, and to whom I was so much indebted. We spent the evening together in love and harmony: and I abandoned entirely, without a moment's hesitation, the idea of leaving a house and family, which were now dearer to me than ever.

The next day, a person was sent to the place of my retreat, to settle all accounts, and to bring back my property. I was taken into still greater favour than formerly; and was never reproached by my parents, for the trouble and anxiety which I had brought upon them. My father probably perceived that I felt sufficiently on the occasion; and he was, perhaps, conscious, that the discipline he had exerted, was not altogether justifiable.—When I reflect on this rash and imprudent adventure; on the miseries in which it might have involved me; and on the singular manner in which I was restored to the bosom of my family; I cannot avoid seeing the hand of Divine Providence in my preservation; and feeling that I ought to be humbly and deeply thankful for the gracious interposition.

Before I quit this subject, I must observe, that soon after I had left home, inquiries were made to discover the place to which I had retreated. I knew that this was the case: but I had made up my mind not to return, and subject myself again to a treatment which I had felt to be improper and unmerited. I therefore declined all the proposals and entreaties of individuals who were friends to the family, and who endeavoured to shake the resolutions I had formed. And I am persuaded that, at this period, nothing would have induced me to relinquish them, but a security against the repetition of the harsh discipline which I had experienced. I rejoice, however, that a train of events so unexpected, and so contrary to my fixed purposes, happily brought me again to the paternal mansion, and settled me safely under its protection.

A short time after I had returned to my father's family, I solicited the privilege of having a private tutor, to instruct me in classical knowledge and liberal studies. With this request, my father very generously complied. A tutor of talents and learning, was procured for me: and I pursued this new career with great alacrity of mind. I sat up late, and rose early, in the prosecution of my studies. In the cold season of the year, I had fuel brought at night into my study, that I might have it ready for kindling a fire at the time of rising, which was frequently before daylight. My tutor was very attentive, and gave me great encouragement to persevere. He stimulated my application, by portraying the advantages of science, and by the commendations which he bestowed on my progress. This close attention to study, and confinement to the house, did not, however, agree with my constitution. My sickly hue proclaimed the intenseness of my application. I found it necessary, therefore, to abate the ardency of my pursuit, and to intermix bodily exercise with my studies. This procedure had a happy effect. I continued regularly employed in my literary occupation; and I could not but be pleased with the advancement I had made, with the augmentation of knowledge, and the improvement of my mental powers.

It is, however, proper to observe, that my attainments under this tutor, were very limited. They served, indeed, to improve my taste, and increase my desire, for learning and knowledge. But this taste and desire were not, at any future period of life, accompanied by that ardour and steadiness of pursuit, which often ensure great success: and my stock of knowledge and literary improvement has, consequently, been always far from extensive.

Though I was a youth of great vivacity, and, by my imprudence and love of pleasure, I had been led into many follies and transgressions; yet I always entertained a high opinion of the enjoyments which piety and virtue bestow; and I venerated the character of those whom I deemed to be truly religious. Such was my opinion of their attainments and happiness, that I probably conceived them to be more exempt from trouble, and more raised above the anxieties of life, than they really were. I knew not the trials of their virtue; the continual watchfulness necessary to resist temptations; their affliction on viewing the crimes and lapses of their fellow-creatures; their sorrowful recollection of their own past offences, joined to the sense of much remaining imperfection; and their solicitude, lest, amidst the changes of the human state, something might, at last, take place, that would prevent their entrance into the mansions of eternal peace. If, indeed, I could have estimated these deductions from the enjoyments of pious and virtuous minds, I believe that I should still have pronounced them the happiest of their species, even in this life: because their satisfactions were of the purest and most elevated kind; and because their troubles arose from the most generous feelings, and were often mingled with the sweetest consolation, and the noblest hopes. This high opinion of the happiness of virtue, and the respectability of its possessors, (which I have never ceased to entertain,) made me listen, with reverence and affection, to their admonitions. Every thing of this nature, and the animated encouragements to a religious life, which I heard from these exemplary persons, whether in public or in private, made a good impression on my mind; and sometimes produced regret, to perceive how distant I was from that felicity, which I believed these good people possessed.

But whatever might be my follies and actual deviations from the line of rectitude, my principles were never disturbed by infidelity or scepticism. I always had the happiness, since I was capable of reflecting on the subject, of having my sentiments fixed in favour of the Christian religion; and no argument that I ever met with, in company or books, had any injurious effects upon me. Some of my acquaintance were either deists or sceptics: but I always found replies to their reasonings, which perfectly satisfied my own mind. This happy persuasion I attribute, under Divine Providence, to my having occasionally looked into, early in life, Leland's View of the Deistical Writers; Butler's Analogy of Religion, Natural and Revealed, to the Constitution and Course of Nature; Sherlock on Providence; and Sherlock's Discourses. These books, with some others, were the means of communicating to my mind, such a survey of the Christian religion and the Divine economy, that I was never much, if at all, embarrassed, by the plausible schemes and objections, which men of prejudiced minds and short-sighted views of religion, had fabricated and produced.—I am firmly persuaded, that the perplexity and doubts, with regard to Christianity and its evidences, which many sensible and well-disposed minds have encountered, and the absolute infidelity of others, may be fairly attributed to the scanty information which they received, on these subjects, during the period of their education, or that by which it was immediately succeeded.

Not long after I had commenced my studies under a private tutor, I entered into a society of young persons, for the purpose of debating on subjects of importance and difficulty, and of exercising ourselves in the art of elocution. The society met weekly; and as the members knew the subject that would be considered at their next meeting, they had opportunity of preparing themselves for the discussion. I generally employed a considerable portion of this preparatory time, in reading books on the question; in reflecting attentively upon it; in collecting the various arguments which bore upon the subject; in considering objections, with the answers to them; and in disposing the whole into some method and order. This institution enlarged my stock of knowledge, promoted the business of arranging my ideas, and probably produced a small degree of correctness and fluency of expression.—These are some of the benefits which result from societies of this nature. But they frequently produce, in young persons, a spirit of disputation and loquacity; and, at least, an inclination to scepticism, even on subjects of great importance. By discovering how much may be plausibly advanced against established truths, and by exerting its ingenuity in support of error, the youthful mind, attracted by the gloss of novelty, and unaccustomed to distinguish between the solid and the superficial, may lose, or abate, its veneration for truth, virtue, and religion.

I scarcely need say, that it is of great consequence to young persons, to have a number of important truths, with the arguments which support them, clearly settled in their minds.

These established principles, as far as they extend, not only satisfy the understanding, and direct, with confidence, the practice of life ; but serve as foundations to support other truths, to the investigation of which the intercourse with men unavoidably leads. If the juvenile mind were duly impressed with truths thus evident and well supported, it would probably acquire such a degree of strength and perspicacity, such a taste for rectitude of sentiment, as would indispose it for the reception of erroneous and sophistical positions. It would, therefore, be highly desirable to cultivate, amongst young persons, such little societies as I have described, for the regular discussion of interesting topics, provided they could be so conducted as to avoid the evils, with which they are too often connected. If these conferences could be managed under the superintendence of respectable persons, whose sound judgment, and comprehensive minds replete with science and literature, would enable them to sum up the arguments advanced, with correctness and liberality ; to give the side of truth the advantages of eloquence and dignity ; and to detect the fallacy of error, and the subtleties of false reasoning ; the benefit of such societies would certainly be obtained with the fewest possible disadvantages. But if this privilege cannot be procured, perhaps the next to it would be, to select, from the members of the society, a few persons the most distinguished for talents, learning, and virtue; who should, by turns, officiate as presidents; and whose special business it should be, to support the cause of truth and reason, and to lay open distinctly every species of sophistry, which might occur in the course of the various discussions. The first of these plans would certainly, in a superior degree, promote order, and inspire a chastened emulation, amongst the members of these little societies. It would, in fact, confer upon them a decorum and respectability, which, in many points of view, would prove highly and permanently advantageous to young persons.

As my mind improved, and my views enlarged, I became still more attached to literary pursuits. I wished for a profession connected with these pursuits; and the study of the law particularly attracted my attention. When I was about seventeen or eighteen years of age, I expressed this inclination to my father: but it met with his decided opposition; and he took great pains to divert my thoughts from the subject. He represented the temptations which I should have to encounter in the practice of the law; and which, he said, would probably lead me to deviate from the principles and conduct of that religious society of which I was a member.

He displayed the advantages I should possess, both in point of emolument and respectability, by the situation in which he was able to place me, as a merchant; and earnestly entreated me to relinquish all prospects of a mode of life, to which there were attached so many difficulties; and to bend my inclinations towards an employment which, I must know, promised almost certain success. I believe I was properly sensible of my father's wishes to establish me advantageously in the world; and of the concern it gave him, to perceive my rooted objection to an occupation, which he very justly considered as both lucrative and honourable. But I found that my inclination was not to be controlled by motives of interest; and though I did not then urge the point, I kept my object steadily in view. After some time had elapsed, I applied myself again vigorously to the subject: but I adopted a new mode of proceeding. I stated the case at large, in writing. My dissatisfaction with the mercantile employment, however beneficial and respectable it might be, and my earnest desire for a literary profession, were fully set forth. All the arguments which I could muster in support of this propensity, and the benefits which it was likely to produce, were enumerated; and every objection which had been advanced against my views and wishes, was distinctly brought forward; and such answers given to the whole, as I thought were satisfactory.

This little performance, which contained several pages, was shown to my father; it was also occasionally shown to some of our friends, particularly to a gentleman of the law, Benjamin Kissam, Esq. who was my father's counsellor, and a man of eminence and integrity in his profession. The statement had a most favourable effect. The counsellor himself became my advocate: and, in a short time, my father consented to place me under his care and tuition. A considerable sum of money was advanced to him by my father as a fee for initiating me, in the business of my new and favourite occupation, and I entered into it with great alacrity. Time now rolled on very pleasantly; and the hope of being settled in a profession adapted to my wishes, gilded my future prospects. After some time, my father very generously presented me with an excellent library, which comprehended both books of law, and some parts of general literature; and which were well calculated to aid and invigorate my studies.—I cannot, however, say that I always found the study of the law to be pleasant. It contains many barren and uninviting tracts, and extensive fields of laborious employment. It abounds with discordant views, with intricate and perplexing discussions, and requires much deep and patient investigation. But I was not discouraged with my occupation. It was the profession of my own choice: it was a respectable business: and it promised to afford me a competent support.

The celebrated John Jay, Esq. late governor of the state of New York, was my fellow student, in the office of our worthy patron, for about two years. His talents and virtues gave, at that period, pleasing indications of future eminence. He was remarkable for strong reasoning powers, comprehensive views, indefatigable application, and uncommon firmness of mind. With these qualifications, added to a just taste in literature, and ample stores of learning and knowledge, he was happily prepared to enter on that career of public virtue, by which he was afterwards honourably distinguished, and made instrumental in promoting the good of his country. This meritorious person, after having occupied some of the highest stations, which the United States could confer upon him, and having lived to see his country abounding in men of eminence and talents, conceived it to be allowable for him, perhaps his duty, to withdraw from the fatigues of office, the contests and anxieties of public life. As a private country gentleman, he has lived on his estate, not far from the city of New York, for many years. Here, in the bosom of an amiable family, and in useful private occupations, he has, I trust, enjoyed that tranquillity which he sought. I hope, that whilst the past affords him many pleasing recollections, and the future is contemplated with composure, the evening of his life will be brightened with the most cheering and animating prospects. This tribute to the merit of an old friend, will not, I believe, be deemed an impertinent digression from the work in which I am engaged.—To the regular progress of that work, I now return.

After four years from the commencement of my law studies, in the office of my truly respectable instructer, I was called to the bar; and received a license to practise, both as counsel and attorney, according to the custom of that time, in all the courts of the province of New York. I soon commenced business, and prosecuted it with success. It answered the expectations I had formed; and I believe my family and friends were satisfied with the prospects which attended me.

Before I entered into business, and about the twentieth year of my age, I conceived a strong attachment and affection for a young woman of personal attractions, good sense, a most amiable disposition, and of a worthy and respectable family. It was not long, before I perceived that my regard met with a favourable reception. Time, and opportunity of knowing each other, confirmed our attachment ; and after two years' acquaintance, we had the satisfaction of being united in the tender bonds of marriage.

We have lived together more than forty years ; and through the whole course of that period, she has been to me a truly affectionate and excellent wife. In all our varied conditions of life, I have received from her the most unequivocal proofs of attachment, and solicitude for my welfare. During my long confinement, on account of bodily infirmities, she has cheerfully met our privations ; tenderly sympathized with me ; and been cordially disposed to forego her own ease, to afford me assistance and comfort. She has, indeed, been a great blessing to me ; and I have abundant cause to be deeply thankful to God, for this unmerited favour, and its continuance to the present time. It yields me great satisfaction, to perceive that our esteem and love for each other, have not diminished with advancing years. The evening of our day has, indeed, been illumined by brighter rays, than those which our morning or meridian light afforded. And I earnestly hope, that, whilst life remains, we shall be favoured, by Divine Grace, to cherish those sentiments and virtues, which will exalt the happiness of our union; support us under every trial; and prepare our minds for the enjoyment of a better world.

I now finish this letter,

And remain,

With sincere regard, &c.

LETTER III.

My dear Friend,

THE two most important events of a man's life, are generally those of his entering into business for himself, and his forming the connexion of marriage. When these events are auspicious, and especially when interest is not too earnestly pursued, there is great reason to look for success, and a good portion of enjoyment through life, provided that correct principles and virtuous habits accompany them. I have already observed, that my marriage was happy, and my business promising: and as our connexions were respectable, and disposed to promote our welfare, I had much to make me thankful to Divine Providence, and to encourage me to persevere in a course of industry and usefulness. I was not influenced by the desire of acquiring great property, and was therefore not disturbed by the cares and anxieties which too often accompany that disposition.

Not long after I had commenced business, some circumstances rendered it proper for me to make a voyage to England; where my father had been about a year on commercial matters of importance, which made his presence there, at that time, very expedient. For many years previous to his leaving America, he had been considerably indisposed: at the best, his constitution was but delicate. The climate of England, however, proved very beneficial. I found him so much improved in his general health, that I could not but wish that he would continue in this country for a few years: and he was so strongly impressed with the hope of receiving benefit, by such a residence, as well as by the advantages which would result to his concerns in trade, that he communicated his views to my mother, and expressed his wish to see her and his children in England. They accordingly, in the course of a few months, came to him: and as I did not expect to return very soon, my wife was persuaded to accompany them across the Atlantic. I had therefore the comfort and satisfaction of meeting again my beloved wife, mother, brother, and sisters. The whole family, thus met together, in a country so distant from their native shores, could not but feel themselves highly gratified, and peculiarly attached to one another. My dear mother was sensible of the improved state of my father's health ; and cheerfully consented to reside a few years in England, for its complete establishment.

When I first came to this country, I had not fixed any time for my continuance in it: but soon after my arrival, it appeared probable that, in the course of a year, I should return to America. There was not, therefore, much opportunity for my dear partner and myself to gratify our curiosity, in surveying what was instructive and interesting in this highly cultivated and happy land. We, however, made a good use of our time; and were much pleased with the novelty and information, which, on every side, continually pressed for attention. It was a peculiar gratification to me, that in these excursions and surveys, I had the society of one, in whose entertainment and instruction I felt myself warmly interested. Every enjoyment was, I believe, heightened to both of us, by the consciousness of each other's participation.

In the latter part of the year 1771, we returned to New York. My parents and the rest of the family remained in England several years. But after this period of trial, my father perceived, that the benefit which he derived from the change of climate, was only temporary. His former indisposition resumed its wonted strength. Having therefore arranged his mercantile affairs entirely to his satisfaction, he, with his family, embarked for New York; and arrived safely there, in the year 1775.

With regard to myself, I observe that, on my return to New York, I resumed the practice of the law. I had many friends and connexions; which renewed the pleasing hopes I had formerly possessed, of succeeding in business. Attention and industry were not wanting; and I enjoyed myself in again settling to my profession. An event, however, occurred at this time, which threatened a diminution of my business, particularly among the society of which I was a member. This society had lately purchased in the city, a valuable piece of ground, for the purpose of erecting upon it a large meeting house, for Divine worship. I was employed to prepare the deed of conveyance. I found every thing regular, drew up the instrument, and, when it was engrossed, delivered it to the trustees, for their inspection before it was executed. When I expected the completion of this business, one of the trustees called upon me, and delicately observed, that in consequence of some doubt as to the validity of the instrument, they had applied to a lawyer of distinction and long established practice, who declared that the conveyance was void, being liable to the statutes of mortmain. I was greatly surprised and hurt; and clearly perceived, that if this opinion were not effectually counteracted, it would strike deeply at my reputation and practice as a lawyer. I therefore desired the person to leave the instrument with me, for a little time, when, I doubted not, I should be able to satisfy the trustees, that it was perfectly regular. I immediately laid the conveyance before the first counsellor in the province, and requested his opinion of it in writing. He gave it, in the most explicit language, and fully adapted to the case. It was, he said, in every respect, a good deed ; and he observed, in particular, that none of the statutes of mortmain would affect it. My mind was completely relieved by this decision. I produced the opinion to the trustees, who were perfectly satisfied with it ; and appeared to be much pleased, that I had so happily extricated myself from the difficulty. The result of this affair was exactly the reverse of what might at first have been expected. It established my reputation among the members of the society. My business increased ; and they applied to me with confidence.

In the practice of the law, pecuniary interest was not my only rule of action. When circumstances would properly admit of it, I generally endeavoured to persuade the person who was threatened with a prosecution, to pay the debt, or make satisfaction, without the trouble and expense of a suit. In doubtful cases, I frequently recommended a settlement of differences, by arbitration, as the mode which I conceived would ultimately prove most satisfactory to both parties. I do not recollect that I ever encouraged a client to proceed at law, when I thought his cause was unjust or indefensible: but, in such cases, I believe it was my invariable practice to discourage litigation, and to recommend a peaceable settlement of differences. In the retrospect of this mode of practice, I have always had great satisfaction; and I am persuaded that a different procedure, would have been the source of many painful recollections.

My business was very successful, and continued to increase till the troubles in America commenced. A general failure of proceedings in the courts of law, then took place. This circumstance, joined to a severe illness, which had left me in a feeble state of health, induced me to remove into the country. We chose for our retreat a situation on Long Island, in the district of Islip, about forty miles from the city of New York. Here we concluded to remain, till the political storm should blow over, and the horizon become again clear and settled. This we did not expect would be very soon; and therefore made our settlement accordingly. As our place of residence was on the borders of a large bay near the ocean, I purchased a very convenient, little pleasure-boat; which I thought would not only amuse me, but contribute to the reestablishment of my health. In this situation, I became extremely attached to the pleasures of shooting, and fishing, and sailing in the bay. These exercises probably gained for me an accession of health and strength; and on that ground, partly reconciled me to an occupation of my time, which was but little connected with mental improvement. I have, however, often regretted that so long a period should have elapsed, without any vigorous application to study; and without an improved preparation for the return of those settled times, when I should again derive my support from the funds of knowledge and judgment. The loss which I sustained, by not sufficiently attending, at this time, to literary pursuits and professional studies, cannot easily be calculated. Every expansion of the mind, every useful habit, and portion of knowledge, at that age especially, is not only so much present gain, but serves as a principal to produce an ever growing and accumulating interest through life. If this advantage were duly appreciated by young persons, it would prove a most powerful stimulus to embrace every proper opportunity, to enlarge the understanding, and to store it with useful knowledge.

On this occasion, I must add, that the recollection of the time which I spent, in the pleasures of shooting, and idly sailing about the bay, affords me no solid satisfaction, in a moral and religious point of view. That time, or the greater part of it, might have been employed, in doing good to others, in the society and converse of pious and virtuous persons, and in the perusal of the sacred volume, and other religious books, tending to establish the heart and life, in the love and practice of goodness. I might have so occupied myself, as to have made my most important interests coincide with my health and bodily enjoyments, instead of indulging myself in that dissipation of mind, and those selfish, injurious habits, which the amusements I had adopted are too apt to produce. I do not, however, wish to censure the practice of other persons in pursuits and amusements with which they are well and conscientiously satisfied. My object is, to state my own feelings and regrets, on the retrospect of this part of my life.

But occupied as I was with amusement, my mind was not so much attached to it, as to be totally inattentive to every thing of a useful nature. About a year after my residence at Islip, the country became greatly distressed from the scarcity of salt. The British cruisers effectually prevented the introduction of that article among the Americans. And the Congress found it necessary to recommend and encourage the making of it, in every place that was favourably situated for the manufacture. I conceived that salt works might be advantageously erected on an island in the bay near which I resided; and I communicated this idea to an ingenious and spirited young man who was my neighbour. He very readily came into the plan, and joined me in the execution of it. We embraced the scheme the more cordially, because we were attached to our country, and felt for the distresses in which it was involved. We procured materials at a considerable expense, employed artificers to construct the works, and were just ready to begin the manufacture, and reap the fruit of our labours, when the British forces took possession of New York, and consequently of Long Island. This event entirely superseded our operations; as the article of salt was then abundantly introduced into the country. Our loss was considerable: but we had no remedy; and the whole concern was, therefore, without hesitation abandoned.

The employment which I had, in devising and superintending these works, was not, however, wholly destitute of advantage to me. The motives which led to it would bear reflection; the occupation of mind and body to which it contributed, was salutary; and the knowledge which I acquired of the business, made some addition to my little stock. I had occasion too, in this event, for the exercise of that virtue, which submits cheerfully to disappointments. This, indeed, was not, in the present instance, an exercise of much difficulty. I was not naturally disposed to brood over misfortunes: but possessed a facility, in turning from the view of them, and presenting to myself objects of a different complexion. This is a propensity which, under proper limitations and government, is doubtless a happy constitution. But, though generally beneficial, I have often indulged it beyond those limits which wisdom prescribes.—A habit of mind that is ever seeking for, and presenting, pleasant objects; and which refuses to contemplate occasionally the disasters and the troubles incident to humanity; nourishes a light and frivolous temper, and prevents the good effects of those salutary lessons, which the adverse occurrences of life, when properly considered, are calculated to produce.

After we had resided at Islip about four years, I became dissatisfied with a mode of life, which consisted chiefly in amusement and bodily exercise. I perceived the necessity of doing something that would provide permanent funds for the expenses of my family. The British power was still maintained at New York, and appeared likely to be established there: and the practice of the law was completely superseded. I had, therefore, no prospect of any considerable employment, but by settling at New York, and entering into mercantile concerns. We removed accordingly to the city, and took a situation favourable for business. My father very generously gave me an unlimited credit, in the importation of merchandise from London: and after forming the best judgment I could of the articles likely to be in demand, I made out a large order. The goods arrived, and I found a ready sale for them. Thus encouraged, I continued to import more of them, and that extensively, every season; and soon perceived that I had engaged in a very lucrative occupation. Every year added to my capital, till, about the period of the establishment of American independence, I found myself able to gratify our favourite wishes, and retire from business.

I purchased a country seat on the banks of the river, about three miles from the city of New York. Here we promised ourselves every enjoyment that our hearts desired. Bellevue, for that was the name of our retreat, was most delightfully situated. A noble river, a mile in breadth, spread itself before us: a rich and pleasant country was on the opposite shore: and our view extended several miles both up and down the river. On this grand expanse of water, vessels and boats of various descriptions, were almost continually sailing. The house was neat and commodious; and accommodated with a spacious and elegant piazza, sashed with Venetian blinds; which added to its coolness in summer, and produced a most soothing and grateful effect. At the back of the mansion, was a large garden, well supplied with fruit, flowers, and useful vegetables: and in other directions from the house, were rows of various kinds of fruit trees, distinguished by their beauty and utility. In the rear of the house and garden, was a pleasant and fertile field, which afforded pasturage for the cattle. This little paradisiacal spot was perfectly to our wishes. Here we fondly hoped often to see our dearest connexions, and to entertain our friends. Every comfort to be derived from useful and interesting society, would, we imagined, be heightened in this pleasing abode. I thought too, that this retreat would be friendly to study, and mental acquisitions; that my health would be improved, by the exercise which I should have in rural occupations; and that the vicinity of the city, and its various institutions, would afford me opportunities of being useful to my fellow-citizens. These hopes and views appeared to be rational and well founded; and I felt no reluctance, or compunction, in indulging them. But the pleasant prospects were soon overcast: the cup of promised sweets was not allowed to approach our lips. Divine Providence had allotted for us a different situation: and I have no doubt that the allotment was both wise and good; and better for us than our own fond appointments.

Before we removed to Bellevue, I had a severe fit of illness, which left me in a very infirm and debilitated state of body. The tone of my muscles was so much impaired, that I could walk but little; and this relaxation continued to increase. I was, besides, in the course of the day, frequently affected with singular sensations of chilness, succeeded by a degree of fever. My situation, at times, became very distressing. I was, however, encouraged by the hope, that a short residence at our delightful retreat, would restore me to my usual state of health and strength. But season succeeded season, without my receiving any salutary effect. I evidently grew worse: and my friends became alarmed at my situation. They generally recommended travelling. Additional exercise, new scenes, and drinking the waters of certain medicinal springs, were thought likely to afford me assistance. As my spirits were good, and life and health very desirable, I cordially entered into the views of my friends; and, with my affectionate and sympathizing partner, I set off for Bristol, in Pennsylvania. We remained in this rural and pleasant town a few weeks: during which time, I bathed, and drank the water; but without any good effect. The weather then growing extremely hot, Farenheit's thermometer being at ninety degrees, we proceeded to some celebrated springs in the mountains of New Jersey. Here, I seemed to grow better for a few weeks: but the water yielded no permanent benefit. From the very elevated situation of those mountains, the air was cool and refreshing: but as the roads were stony and broken, I could not have the advantage of regular exercise in a carriage. To remedy this inconvenience, I made some efforts on horseback, and some on foot: but these efforts fatigued me to a great degree, and increased the debility under which I laboured.

Perceiving that neither the springs, nor the situation, produced any beneficial effects; and travelling being one of the means for the recovery of health, which had been recommended to me; we left the mountains, and bent our course towards Bethlehem, in Pennsylvania, a healthful and pleasant town about fifty miles from Philadelphia. This is a settlement of the Moravians. The situation of the place, its refreshing and salutary air, joined to the character of its inhabitants, made a cheering impression upon us ; and we took up our quarters at the inn with pleasure, and with the hope of advantage. A few days after we had settled here, we were most agreeably surprised, by the arrival of my father, and my sister Beulah. This affectionate parent had long been anxious about my health, and solicitous to promote it. And perceiving that we were not likely to return very soon, and that I had not received much benefit, he was desirous of spending a little time with us ; which he naturally thought would have a cheering effect on his children, in their present solitary excursion. This visit was as grateful as it was unexpected. My sister was a sensible and amiable young woman, of a gentle nature and engaging manners, to whom we were both very nearly attached: we therefore formed a little band, closely united by the ties of affection and consanguinity. This pleasing association, joined to the beauty and retirement of the place, gave an animating impulse to my spirits ; so that I was better at Bethlehem than I had been in any other part of the journey.

There was here much to occupy the mind, and to gratify curiosity. The different houses appropriated to the single brethren, the single sisters, and the widows, with the various economy of the society, were subjects of an interesting nature. The

spirit of moderation, the government of the passions, and the tranquillity and happiness, which appeared to pervade every part of this retired settlement, made on our minds a strong and pleasing impression. We several times visited the different departments; and, at our inn, received occasionally the visits of a number of their most respectable members. They were very communicative; and attended with liberality and good humour, to the ideas which we suggested, for the improvement of particular parts of their economy. Among other observations, we took occasion to inquire, whether the practice of the elders and elderesses in selecting a partner for a young man who wished to marry, was not sometimes attended with serious inconveniences. But they seemed to have no doubt, that this regulation produced more happy marriages, than would be effected by leaving the parties to choose for themselves. A lively and sensible person, with whose conversation we were particularly pleased, took occasion to give us his own experience on the subject. He expressed himself to the following effect. "When I wished to change my situation in life, I applied to one of our elders, and communicated the matter to him. He asked me whether I had any particular young woman in view. I replied in the negative; and that I wished my superiors to choose for me. Pleased with my answer, and the confidence reposed in them, he assured me that the greatest care should be taken, to select for me a partner, who would be, in every respect, proper for me. The elders and elderesses consulted together, and, after a suitable time, fixed on a young woman, whose disposition and qualifications were correspondent to my own, and which they thought were adapted to make me happy. We were introduced to each other, in the presence of our superiors. The interview was favourable: we became mutually attached; and, in a short time, we were married. The event has perfectly answered our most sanguine hopes. I probably should not have chosen so happily, if I had been left to decide for myself; but I am certain I could not have made a better choice." He concluded his observations with a degree of animation and satisfaction, which precluded all doubt of the truth of his assertions.

The roads and scenery about Bethlehem were very delightful. I frequently enjoyed the pleasure they afforded, by riding in a small open carriage, which gave me a good opportunity of surveying the beauties of the country. In one of these excursions, I observed a gate which opened into some grounds that were very picturesque. Without proper consideration, I desired the servant who accompanied me, to open the gate. Almost immediately I observed a group of cheerful, neatly dressed young females approaching. They had been gathering blackberries, a rich fruit in that country; and each of them had a little basket in her hand filled with this sort of fruit. I soon perceived that I had committed a trespass, in offéring to enter the grounds appropriated entirely to the walks of females. When they came near me, I apologized for the intrusion, by alleging that I did not know the peculiar use to which the enclosure was applied. With great good nature, and genuine politeness, some of them intimated that I was perfectly excusable. I believe the number of this cheerful group was about thirty, between the ages of fifteen and twenty-five. The sight of so much apparent innocence and happiness was extremely pleasing. And whilst they stood near the carriage, from which I could not conveniently alight, I thought it would be proper to express my respect and good wishes for them. I therefore took the liberty of addressing them in a short speech; which, as near as I can recollect, was to the following purport. I observed that it gave me particular pleasure, to see them all so happy: that their situation was, indeed, enviable, and singularly adapted to produce much real enjoyment, and to protect them from the follies, the vices, and the miseries, of the world: that if they knew the troubles and exposures, which are to be met with in the general intercourse of life, they would doubly enjoy their safe and tranquil seclusion from those dangers, and be thankful for the privileges they possessed. My harangue seemed to have a good effect upon them. They smiled, and some of them said that they were indeed happy in their situation. A few of them then held up their little baskets, and desired I would help myself to some fruit. I thanked them; and took more than I wanted, that I might the better gratify their benevolence. I then parted with this pleasing company, and pursued another road, well satisfied with a mistake and adventure which had yielded me so much heart-felt satisfaction.

I must not omit to mention, that these good young persons reported to their superiors the whole of this transaction, with what had been said on the occasion. But I found that, notwithstanding my intrusion, I had lost no credit with the elderesses. For they sent to inform the sick gentleman, (this was the term by which I was designated,) that he had full liberty, and was welcome, whenever he chose, to ride in the grounds appropriated to the walks of the females. I acknowledged the favour of so great a privilege; but as I could not think it entirely warrantable and proper to make use of it, I never repeated my visit to this interesting place.

Of the various institutions of this settlement, we particularly admired that for the benefit of widows. This house met our entire approbation. An asylum for those who had lost their most valuable earthly treasures, and who could neither receive from the world, nor confer upon it, much, if any, important service, appeared to have a just foundation in wisdom and benevolence. But to detach from many of the advantages and duties of society, young persons in the full possession of health, strength, and spirits, seemed to us, on the whole view of the subject, a very questionable policy; though certainly some very important moral uses were derived from the institutions which respected the single brethren and the single sisters.—Having formed some acquaintance with several worthy persons in this happy town, and being much gratified with our visit, we took our leave with regret. I cannot easily forget the pleasing impressions which this settlement left upon my mind. The grandeur of the neighbouring hills; the winding course of its adjacent beautiful river; and the serene, enlivening state of the atmosphere; joined to the modest and tranquil appearance of the inhabitants; their frequent and devout performance of Divine worship; and their unaffected politeness and good humour; are sufficient to render Bethlehem a most interesting and delightful retreat. To the calm and soothing virtues of life, it is, certainly, a situation peculiarly favourable. But the moral excellences, connected with arduous and dignified exertion, meet, perhaps, with but few occasions here to call them forth.

After we left Bethlehem, where we had spent several weeks, it seemed expedient to bend our course towards home. My father was affected with fresh symptoms of a disorder to which he had been long subject; and he thought it would not be prudent to continue his visit any longer. Under these circumstances, we could not suffer him and my sister to proceed on their journey alone. Had he been as well as usual, it would have been very agreeable to us to have remained longer at Bethlehem; and particularly to have visited the place of my nativity, which was about fifty miles further in the interior of the country. This visit we had all contemplated; and purposed to set off for the place in a few days. But my father's sudden indisposition made it necessary to relinquish our views entirely. Had we executed our purpose, I have no doubt that the visit would have been to me peculiarly interesting, and attended with emotions of a pleasing and serious nature; and I could not, indeed, avoid anticipating them in some degree. To have viewed the spot, where I first felt the blessings of existence; and where my dear parents had extended their early cares over me, and had commenced their settlement in life; must have excited in me sensations highly gratifying. To have reflected on the superintendence of Divine Providence, from the first hour of my existence, through a period of nearly forty years; on the numberless preservations from danger, which, through that course of time, had threatened my life, or my happiness; and on the many positive blessings with which I had so long been favoured; could not, I believe, have failed to excite a lively and extraordinary sense of the unmerited goodness of God to me; and would probably have proved a peculiarly animating source of humble and grateful recollection.—But how pleasing and useful soever this visit to Swetara might have been, prudence required us to give it up; and we proceeded, by easy stages, towards New York. There we safely arrived, after an agreeable journey; in which my father's health had not materially suffered, by the fatigue and exposure which he encountered, and which to him were unusual.

This seems to be a proper stage for closing the present letter. My next will enter on a period, which was particularly interesting to me, and which was occupied in a manner very different from my expectations.

I am, with due respect, &c.

LETTER IV.

My dear Friend,

It is a common and just observation, that the blessings of this life, however numerous and important, lose their relish, when we are deprived of health. Many of them are then imbittered, and others are totally disregarded. We are therefore naturally solicitous to recover a possession so pleasing in itself, and so necessary to the enjoyment of other pleasures. I was the more sensible of the value of this blessing, because I had lost it; and because I possessed many others, which I found were, in a great degree, dependent upon this. I thought, indeed, that nothing besides this desirable object, was wanting, to render me very happy. But, without doubt, I deceived myself, in the indulgence of this fond sentiment. Had I possessed health, joined to all the means of happiness with which I was surrounded, it is probable that some unforeseen event, something in myself, or in others with whom I was connected, would soon have overcast the pleasant scene; and convinced me practically, that unmixed enjoyment does not belong to this state of existence.—There is, however, enough to be enjoyed; enough to make us truly thankful to Divine Providence. I was therefore anxious for my recovery, and omitted no promising means to obtain it, whilst life was yet in its prime, and the value of health was proportionably enhanced.

When we were again settled at Bellevue, we had rather mournfully to reflect on the little benefit, if any, which my health had derived from our summer excursion; and we naturally turned our attention to other means of relief that might promise success. During the course of my indisposition, I had found that I was generally better when the weather was cold: a temporary bracing was commonly the effect of the winter season. But we had observed that every succeeding summer took from me more than the winter had given. The prospect was therefore discouraging. Under these circumstances, I consulted one of the first physicians of the country, who happened at that time to be at New York. He paid a friendly attention to my situation: and after maturely considering the case, advised me to remove to a climate, where the summers are more temperate, and less relaxing; and where, consequently, I might not lose, in warm weather, the bracing effects produced by the rigours of winter. From what he knew of Yorkshire, in England, he thought some parts of it might prove a proper situation. On the whole, he recommended to me, in a sensible and affectionate letter which I received from him, to make the experiment; and he expressed an earnest hope, that it might be blessed with success. He thought that my disorder was of such a nature, that medicines would not be proper for me: "at any rate," he said, "I would advise you not to take much medicine." This advice was consonant with the views and practice which I had long adopted; and confirmed me in my determination. For more than twenty years, I have almost entirely declined the use of medicines: and to this I attribute, in a great measure, the good appetite, and unbroken rest at nights, which, during that period, I have generally enjoyed. The natural tone of my stomach has not been injured by the operation of drugs, nor any new disorder superinduced. I, however, think that medicines are sometimes of great use: the discovery and due application of them, are a blessing to mankind. In my particular case, they would, I believe, have been injurious.

After deliberately considering the advice of my physician, and the importance of the undertaking, we were fully convinced that it was expedient to try the effect of a more favourable climate, and to make a short residence in England. Dear as were our relatives and friends, and our native land, we resolved to forego the enjoyment of them. But hope cheered us with the prospect, that the separation would not be long; and that we should return to them, with renewed health and spirits, and capacities of greater happiness in their society. My dear wife did not hesitate a moment, in resolving to accompany me to a distant country; and to render me every aid, which her affection, and solicitude for my happiness, could suggest.

Soon after our determination was made, we prepared for the voyage. The trying scene now commenced of taking leave of our relations and friends. Many of them accompanied us to the ship, in the cabin of which we had a most solemn parting. An eminent minister was present at this time, for whom we had a particular esteem and regard, and who prayed fervently on the occasion. It was a deeply affecting time; and, I trust, produced salutary impressions on all our minds. Our feelings, at the moment of separation, may be more easily conceived than described. But satisfied with the propriety of our undertaking, and consoled by the hope of success, our minds gradually became tranquil and resigned. With many, if not with all, of those beloved connexions, we parted never to see them again, in this life: for many of them have since been translated to the world of spirits. But we humbly trust, that the separation will not be perpetual: that, through redeeming mercy and love, we shall be again united to virtuous connexions, and happily join with them, and the blessed of all generations, in glorifying our heavenly Father, and joyfully serving him for ever, with enlarged minds and purified affections.

We embarked in a commodious ship, near the close of the year 1784; and, after a prosperous voyage of about five weeks, landed at Lymington. Near the conclusion of the voyage, we narrowly escaped some very dangerous rocks, which would, in all probability, have proved fatal to us, if we had struck upon them. Thus preserved by the care of a gracious Providence, we had fresh cause to be humbly thankful to God, and to be encouraged to trust in his goodness, for future preservation and direction.

In contemplating the place where we were to reside, during our continuance in England, it was our frequent and special desire, that our lot might be cast in the neighbourhood and society of religious and exemplary persons; from whom we might derive encouragement to the practice of virtue. We had lived long enough to perceive, how strongly the human mind is influenced, and how apt it is to be moulded, by the dispositions and pursuits of those with whom it is intimately connected. We had felt the danger of intercourse with persons, who seemed to make the pleasures of this life the great object of their attention; and we had derived comfort, and some degree of religious strength, from the society and example of good and pious persons. In this desire of being settled favourably for the cultivation of our best interests, we had the happiness of being gratified; and we consider this privilege, which we have now enjoyed for more than twenty years, as one of the greatest blessings of our lives.

It may not be improper to mention in this place, that when we left our native shores, we fondly supposed, that in the course of two years, my health might be so established, as to enable us to return to our friends and country. This term was the utmost boundary we had assigned for our absence from home. How short-sighted is the mind of man! How little do we know of the future, and of the events which are to occupy it! Two and twenty years have passed away since we left our native land, and little hope remains of our ever being able to visit it again. But resignation is our duty. And this should be the more cheerful, as we have been so long preserved together by Divine Providence, in this happy country; where we have been abundantly blessed, and for which we can never be sufficiently grateful.

Our attachment to England was founded on many pleasing associations. In particular, I had strong prepossessions in favour of a residence in this country; because I was ever partial to its political constitution, and the mildness and wisdom of its general system of laws. I knew that, under this excellent government, life, property, reputation, civil and religious liberty, are happily protected; and that the general character and virtue of its inhabitants, take their complexion from the nature of their constitution and laws. On leaving my native country, there was not, therefore, any land, on which I could cast my eyes with so much pleasure; nor is there any, which could have afforded me so much real satisfaction, as I have found in Great Britain.—May its political fabric, which has stood the test of ages, and long attracted the admiration of the world, be supported and perpetuated by Divine Providence! And may the hearts of Britons be grateful for this blessing, and for many others by which they are eminently distinguished!

I now return to the narrative. In a few days after our landing, we reached London. Here we were cheered with the society of a number of our friends, whom we had known, in the visit which we made to this country in the year 1771.

We continued in and near London about six weeks; and then proceeded for Yorkshire. Some of our friends advised us to fix our residence at Pontefract, others at Knaresborough, and others at Richmond, Settle, or upon the Wolds. We, however, thought it prudent to visit a number of places, before we concluded to fix upon any one. At length we came to York: and whether we were influenced by the association of names, by the pleasantness of the surrounding country, or by other motives, we felt some partiality for the place. But it appeared to be difficult to procure a suitable residence in the vicinity: and we left York to visit Knaresborough, Harrogate, and the neighbourhood of Leeds. Soon after we had set off, we observed, about a mile from the city, in a small village called Holdgate, a house and garden very pleasantly and healthfully situated. The place struck our minds so agreeably, that we stopped the carriage, for a few minutes, to survey it. The more we observed the house and its appendages, the more we liked them; and we concluded that if they could be obtained, they would suit us better than any other we had seen. With this reflection, we passed on, and continued our journey. At Knaresborough and Harrogate, we stayed a short time: but neither of these places appeared to coincide with our views, and we went forward to Leeds. From this place, I wrote to a friend at York, and requested him to inquire, whether the house near that city, which had so pleasantly impressed us, could be either hired or purchased, and on what terms. My friend informed me, that the owner of this estate resided upon it, that he had considerably improved it, and that it was perfectly to his mind; so that he intended to occupy it for the remainder of his life. All prospect of acquiring this situation being thus cut off, we employed ourselves in looking at several places near Leeds. But our attachment to York still continued, and after several weeks' absence from it, we returned, with the hope that some suitable place, in the neighbourhood of this city, would yet be found. That we might have the fairer opportunity for selecting such a residence, I hired for six months a house ready-furnished, in York; and occasionally made inquiry for a situation in its vicinity. About five months of the time elapsed before any place occurred, which was adapted to our wishes. At this period, the house and premises which had appeared to us so desirable, were advertised for sale. The owner, who was an officer in the navy, had unexpectedly an offer made to him of a ship on a remote station; and being pleased with the appointment, he concluded to take his family with him, and to dispose of his property at Holdgate. I did not hesitate to apply as a purchaser; and, in a short time, the contract was made, and the estate secured to me. We soon removed into our new residence; and found it to answer, in every respect, the expectations we had formed. It is healthy, pleasant, commodious, and unites the advantages of both town and country. This little pleasing settlement, has lost none of its comforts in our view, though we have now enjoyed it two and twenty years. I hope that I have not dwelt too long, on the circumstance of selecting a residence at Holdgate. This place has been our habitation, for so great a portion of our lives, and has contributed so much to our comfort and enjoyment, that I could not pass over the recital, without some marked attention. I cannot but trace, and gratefully acknowledge, the goodness of Divine Providence, in the circumstances which led us to this auspicious residence.

Though I have described the house and garden at Holdgate, as a desirable possession, yet it is by no means a large or a showy one. It is, however, one that accords with our own taste and desires. My views and wishes, with regard to property, were, in every period of life, contained within a very moderate compass. I was early persuaded that, though "a competence is vital to content," I ought not to annex to that term the idea of much property. And I determined that when I should acquire enough to enable me to maintain and provide for my family, in a respectable and moderate manner, and this according to real and rational, not imaginary and fantastic wants, and a little to spare for the necessities of others ; I would decline the pursuits of property, and devote a great part of my time, in some way or other, to the benefit of my fellow-creatures, within the sphere of my abilities to serve them. I perceived that the desire of great possessions, generally expands with the gradual acquisition, and the full attainment, of them : and I imagined, that charity and a generous application, do not sufficiently correspond with the increase of property. I thought too, that procuring great wealth, has a tendency to produce an elated independence of mind, little connected with that humility, which is the ground of all our virtues ; that a busy and anxious pursuit of it, often excludes views and reflections of infinite importance, and leaves but little time to acquire that treasure, which would make us rich indeed. I was inclined to think, that a wish for personal distinction, a desire of providing too abundantly for their children, and a powerful habit of accumulation, are the motives which commonly actuate men, in the acquisition of great wealth. The strenuous endeavours of many persons to vindicate this pursuit, on the ground, that the idea of a competency is indefinite, and that the more we gain, the more good we may do with it, did not make much impression upon me. I fancied that, in general, experience did not correspond with this plausible reasoning; and I was persuaded that a truly sincere mind could be at no loss to discern the just limits between a safe and competent portion, and a dangerous profusion, of the good things of life. These views of the subject, I reduced to practice; and terminated my mercantile concerns, when I had acquired a moderate competency.

By what I have said on this occasion, I do not mean to cast any reflection on the prudent efforts of persons, who have large families to support, and provide for; or who, instead of adding to the superfluous heap, apply their gains to the relief of want, the instruction of ignorance, or, in any other way, to the substantial benefit of their fellow-creatures. I am, indeed, far from being disposed to censure or disapprove the exertions of such persons, in the steady pursuit of business, and the acquisition of property. My view, in the remarks which I have made on this topic, is, rather to justify my own determination to withdraw seasonably from the pursuit of property, than to reflect on the conduct of those who, with proper inducements, think it their duty to endeavour to enlarge their possessions. This is a subject, on which it is certainly more charitable and becoming, to suggest hints, for the consideration of others, when we may have occasion, and think it prudent, so to do, than presumptuously to make decisions, respecting their motives and conduct.

When I first settled at Holdgate, my general health had been, in some degree, improved; and I was able to walk in the garden, without assistance, several times in the course of a day. This increase of strength, and ability to walk out in the open air, were highly pleasing; and gave a fresh spring to our hopes, that the period was not very far distant, when we might return to our native country and our friends, with the blessings of established health, and all the comforts which follow in its train. But these cheering prospects did not long continue. The exercise in my garden was so delightful, and appeared to be so beneficial to me, that I often indulged myself in it; till, at length, I found my little stock of newly acquired strength began to decline, and that the former weakness of the muscles returned. This was not the effect of great and immoderate exertion; but proceeded from my not knowing how very limited my bodily powers were, and from not keeping within those limits. I soon perceived that it was necessary to give up my little excursions in the garden: but I continued to walk occasionally about the room, as much as I was well able to bear, knowing the danger of resigning myself to a state of inactivity. This practice was kept up, in a greater or less degree, till it became inconvenient and painful. A walk even from my seat to the window, at last overcame me, and produced a distressing weariness and fatigue, which pervaded the whole animal system. I occasionally made repeated efforts to overcome these effects: but all to no purpose; the more I persisted in my exertions, the more painful was my situation. I perceived that I was always better, and more at my ease, when I continued sitting. This induced me to try the experiment of relinquishing all attempts at walking, and to keep to my seat through the course of the day. The result was, in every respect, beneficial. The soreness of the muscles abated; the little tone which remained in them, was not disturbed or overstretched; and I enjoyed an easy and tolerable state of health.

I made it a point, however, to ride out daily in my carriage: and this, doubtless, contributed to counteract the injurious effects which would have resulted from constant inaction. The motion of the carriage, the change of scene, differ-

ence of air, and the busy or the cheerful faces of my fellow-creatures, produced a pleasing effect on my mind, and greatly tended to reconcile me to the privation of other exercise. Though I had not sufficient strength to get into a carriage, by the usual method, I have always been able to effect it, by means of a board laid nearly level from the garden gate to the step of the carriage. But I have repeatedly found this exertion to be the full extent of my powers. I can, however, generally accomplish it, with little or no inconvenience. This mode of getting into the carriage, has often excited the curiosity of persons who were passing at the time, and given rise to strange surmises, and to some ridiculous stories. Inability to account for facts is an uneasy state of mind; to get rid of which many people are apt to suppose or admit causes, which, how imaginary soever they may be, are yet sufficient to prevent the trouble of further investigation. I must, however, allow, that, in my own case, the appearance of general health, and the ease with which I moved on the board, might very naturally induce a belief, that I was capable of greater exertions, and that the weakness existed more in the mind than in the body. If, under a change of circumstances, I had been the observer, instead of the person observed, I might very probably have formed a similar judgment.

The state of weakness and confinement to which I was now reduced, would, at some periods of my life, have been almost insupportable. But my infirmities had increased upon me gradually, and I had the happiness to perceive that they might be made to conduce to my future and immortal interests. I had many enjoyments and advantages yet left to me: I was, in general, free from pain; I could take a little daily exercise; my appetite was good; and my rest at nights commonly sound and uninterrupted. I had the society of worthy and intelligent friends, converse with books, and a regular correspondence with my distant connexions. I was able, too, to attend public religious worship, once or twice in the week, which I consider as an invaluable privilege. There still remained to me the great blessing of an affectionate, faithful friend, my beloved wife; whose solicitude to promote my comfort, in all respects, has been lively and uniform, through every period of our union. Thus surrounded with benefits so important, it would have been impious to complain, or to deplore my condition. It became me rather, to number my blessings: and I humbly trust that, through Divine grace, I have been enabled cheerfully to submit to my lot, and to be thankful for the mercies, the unmerited mercies, which have been bestowed upon me.

In the summer of 1786, I met with a great loss, in the decease of my father. He had been painfully affected, with a cough and weakness of the stomach, for more than thirty years; and the disorder at length increased so much, that nature could no longer support the conflict.—In a letter which I received from his brother, my worthy uncle John Murray, there are some circumstances of his death, which are so interesting to me, that they may not improperly be mentioned in this place. The circumstances alluded to, are contained in the following extracts from the letter. "Your much esteemed father departed this life the 22nd of July, 1786, about five o'clock in the afternoon, with all his children in the house, yourself excepted. About four weeks ago, without any apparent cause, but the natural increase of the disorder which he had long had, he was confined to his room, and complained of pain in his head and breast, and that his cough grew more difficult and painful. Soon after, in conversing with him, he told me that his dissolution was near at hand; and he thanked his God, that, in the whole course of his life, he had never found himself so much resigned as at that time; and that it was not his wish to live longer. In this sincere composure of mind he continued, perfectly sensible, till the moment of his death, which took place at my side, and without a groan. About three days before his decease, your letter by the packet came to hand. It was read to him; and finding you were recovered, in some degree, from the relapse you had fallen into, it seemed to afford him real pleasure. He thanked God for all his mercies; and said: 'This is the last time I shall hear from my dear son.'"

Thus peacefully left the world my dear and affectionate father, in the sixty-fifth year of his age; and, I trust, exchanged this life for one infinitely better.

After I left America, my father, during the remainder of his life, kindly transacted all my business; and obliged me with a regular correspondence, from which I derived much comfort and satisfaction. The religious state of mind which his letters demonstrated, under the pressure of years and infirmities, afforded me peculiar pleasure at the time; and continues to be a source of grateful recollection. The loss which I had sustained, in being deprived of my father's kind offices, my truly valuable brother, John Murray, was studious to repair. For more than twenty years, he has attended to my concerns in America; and maintained a correspondence with me, in the most brotherly and affectionate manner. Sympathizing with us, in our long and distant separation from our near connexions and our native country, he has been kindly solicitous to diminish our anxieties, by a great variety of communications. We owe much of our relief and consolation, to his unwearied attention, and to the proofs he has given us of his esteem and love, during our long residence in England. We were affectionately attached to each other, in early life: but this attachment has not only continued, but it has increased with time; and I firmly trust it will remain, and brighten, to the latest period of our lives. From my dear sisters, I have also received, in this long absence, many testimonies of their sincere regard, and solicitude for my welfare. These could not fail of being soothing to us; and they tended to cherish the feelings of mutual affection.

The relation which subsists between children of the same family, and between other persons very nearly connected, is of a peculiarly tender and endearing kind; and it should be cherished, not only as a duty, but as one of the most lively and interesting sources of our enjoyments. It produces and augments affections which may be continually exercised, because their objects are often before us: and, by perpetual offices of love, and solicitude for one another's welfare, it accustoms the heart to these emotions, and prepares it for extending its charities to all around. In this manner, some of the finest feelings of our nature, may be matured; and disposed, on all proper occasions, to expand themselves to objects, far and near, in substantial acts of kindness, compassion, and benevolence.—This expansive nature of the affections, is so aptly and beautifully illustrated by a celebrated poet, that it may not be improper to cite the illustration here.

> "God loves from whole to parts: but human soul
> Must rise from individual to the whole.
> Self-love but serves the virtuous mind to wake,
> As the small pebble stirs the peaceful lake:
> The centre mov'd, a circle straight succeeds,
> Another still, and still another spreads.
> Friend, parent, neighbour, first it will embrace;
> His country next; and next all human race:
> Wide and more wide, th' o'erflowings of the mind
> Take ev'ry creature in, of ev'ry kind.
> Earth smiles around, with boundless bounty bless'd;
> And Heav'n beholds its image in his breast."

But how beneficial soever may be the tendency of this domestic and social intercourse, I am inclined to believe that its happy effects are often limited, and sometimes lost, for want of due reflection and encouragement. Enjoyments which are very familiar, and of daily or hourly occurrence, are apt to pass by us unnoticed: and frequently, from this circumstance, they almost lose their nature, and become nearly, if not altogether, uninteresting. It is therefore of high importance to our virtue and happiness, that we should often call ourselves to account, for the estimate, and the use, we make of the blessings with which we are surrounded. Our self examination, with regard to the subject under consideration, would perhaps be rendered more effectual, by an individual inquiry, how far we have attended to the means of augmenting our domestic and social enjoyments. Inquiries similar to those which follow, seriously put to ourselves, would present these enjoyments in lively and impressive points of view.—Are we duly sensible how happy we really are, in the possession of affectionate relations, and in the constant interchange of kind offices? Do we consider properly, how much we depend on their attachment and love, for the numerous and the daily pleasures we enjoy? how often we have experienced their sympathy and aid, when we have had to encounter affliction or disappointment? and how ready they would be to fly to our assistance again, if we should need their consolation and support? Do we sometimes picture in our minds, the wants and distresses which we should feel, if we were deprived of these tender and faithful friends? and reflect, that when they are lost, they are lost for ever to us in this world?—It is scarcely possible, that repeated examinations of this nature, should not be productive of the happiest effects, by teaching us continually to value and improve our present privileges.—A similar process of reflection, with respect to health of mind and body; a competence of property; fair reputation; civil and religious liberty; the light of Christianity; and exemption from numerous evils; and every other favour conferred upon us by Divine Providence; would not only refine and exalt these blessings in our estimation, but affect our hearts with more fervent gratitude to the Giver of all good, for the continuance of his bounties, both temporal and spiritual.—That I may be much more studious than I ever have been, to number and improve my blessings; and to avoid the reproaches of my own heart, for suffering them to pass by me unacknowledged; is my sincere and earnest desire.

I am, very affectionately, &c.

LETTER V.

My dear Friend,

I HAVE often considered it as a special privilege, demanding my grateful acknowledgments to Divine Providence, that my afflictions have admitted of great alleviation; and that they have been laid upon me, with a most lenient hand. When I became confined, and incapable of but very little bodily exercise, I was not wholly deprived of every species of exertion. I could still employ myself in reading, in writing, and in conversation. My mind was preserved free and active. I might therefore hope to be exercised in doing something that would be useful to myself and others: something that would agreeably employ my mental powers; and prevent that tedium and irritability, which bodily infirmities too often occasion. This might be accomplished in various ways; and I ventured to believe it might, in part, be effected by a publication which I had in view, and which I presumed would be interesting to many readers.

In the early part of my life, as well as in its succeeding periods, I had a lively pleasure and satisfaction, in perusing the sentiments of eminent and virtuous persons, on the subject of religion and futurity, when they approached the close of life. From men who had known the world, and who were qualified, and disposed, to give a true estimate of its nature and enjoyments, and whom we could not suspect of dissimulation at that awful period, much important instruction, I conceived, might be derived; and I trust I have been, in some degree, benefited by studies of this kind. Reflecting on the pleasure, and the good effects, which this species of reading had produced on my own mind, I naturally supposed that it would be attended with similar effects on the minds of others. I thought too, that a collection of the testimonies of great and good persons, in favour of piety and virtue, would, if they were properly arranged, be more interesting, and more efficacious, than a perusal of them detached, as many of them are, in the pages of history and biography. Under these impressions, or views of the subject, I commenced my little work. As I wished to form it on liberal principles, and render it acceptable to readers in general, I was careful to introduce characters of various religious professions, and of different ages and countries. The concurrence of these, in the recommendation of religion, as the great promoter of our happiness here and hereafter, would, I conceived, form a strong persuasive evidence, in the cause of piety and virtue. I flattered myself, that a body of testimonies, so striking and important, would exhibit religion in a most attractive form: and that it would be calculated to console and animate the well-disposed; to rouse the careless; and to convince, or, at least, to discountenance, the unbeliever. In the course of the work, I annexed to many of the characters, such observations as appeared to me to rise out of the subject, and to be calculated to arrest the reader's attention, and promote the design which I had in view.

The first edition of this book, which was entitled, "The Power of Religion on the Mind, &c.," appeared in the year 1787. It consisted of only five hundred copies; all of which were neatly bound, and distributed at my own expense. I sent them to the principal inhabitants of York and its vicinity; and accompanied each book with an anonymous note requesting a favourable acceptance of it, and apologizing for the liberty I had taken. It was not without some hesitation, that I adopted so singular a mode of distribution. But, on mature reflection, I believed it to be more eligible than any other, for the purpose which I had in view. And as I was but little known in the city, and the work was anonymous, I perhaps indulged a hope, that the author might not be recognised, and that the business would pass away, without much, if any, reflection upon me. At any rate, I flattered myself, that if the author should be discovered, the goodness of his intentions, would protect him from the severity of censure, even by those who might be disposed to consider his procedure as rather eccentric.

I soon found that my publication was well received: and it was not long before I was encouraged to print a new edition of the work, in London, which met with a good sale. Several other impressions appeared in different places. When, after some time, a sixth edition was called for, I was induced to enlarge the book, and to put my name to it. And as I afterwards found that it continued to make a favourable progress, I conceived that if the copyright were assigned to some booksellers of extensive business and influence, it would be circulated more diffusively, and my design in composing it be still more effectually answered. Under this idea, I extended the work considerably; made some improvements in the language; and then disposed of the copyright, without any pecuniary recompense. With this plan, I have every reason to be perfectly satisfied. The demand for the book has far exceeded my utmost expectation: and the testimonies of approbation, and of its usefulness, which I have received, have been truly gratifying; and have given me cause to be thankful to the Author of my being, that I have been the instrument, even in a small degree, of disseminating excitements to a pious and virtuous course of life.

I am sensible it is difficult to write with proper delicacy, concerning publications which have been made by one's self; especially if they have been attended with any demonstrations of public favour and respect. I hope, however, that in the preceding account of the "Power of Religion on the Mind," I have not deviated from the dictates of propriety; and that, in the narrative and observations, which I may hereafter make, respecting my other literary productions, I shall be careful to offer nothing which may not be warranted by the occasion, and the nature of the subject. These productions have occupied so material a part of my life, and engaged so much of my study and attention, that I shall not, perhaps, be censured, for dwelling upon them with some degree of particularity.

At the close of the year 1794, I was seized with a severe illness, which continued for many weeks; and reduced me to so feeble a state, that my recovery was much doubted. During the continuance of this affliction, I was often desirous, that, if it were the will of Divine Providence, I might be removed from this state of trouble, and landed safely, as I hoped through Infinite mercy I should be, on those happy shores, where there is neither sickness nor sorrow. But I must acknowledge, that this desire of being released from life, and its attendant trials, was not consistent with that reverence and resignation to the will of God, which are due to him from all his rational creatures. He who notices the fall of every sparrow, sees us in all our afflictions; and knows how to support us under them, and the proper time to deliver us from their pressure; and he will assuredly do what he knows to be best for us. From the greatest distresses, good may proceed: our spirits may receive additional refinement; and our example of pious, humble submission, may be edifying and consoling to our friends and others.

I have, in the course of forty years, been visited with many illnesses, some of which have been very painful, and brought me near the gates of death. But I have always had the happiness to perceive, that they were a necessary and salutary discipline, replete with instruction of the most important nature, and better for me, than if I had enjoyed a uniform tenour of health and strength. In reflecting upon them, I have been so fully convinced of their utility, that I view them as concealed blessings; and have reason to be very grateful to Divine Providence, for this mixture of bitters with the sweets of life.

There are many powerful reasons for our bearing with patience, resignation, and even with cheerfulness, the bodily afflictions with which we are visited. It is the will of God that we should be subject to them. Pain and death are the appointment of Divine Providence, as the lot of man: and therefore, to endure them, with composure and reverence, is our duty. They are designed to let us see our weakness; the insufficiency of the things of time to make us happy; and the necessity of providing for a better state.—They tend to refine our minds, to exalt our views, and prepare us for future happiness. "These light afflictions, which are but for a moment, work for us a far more exceeding and eternal weight of glory."—They form a part of the punishment for sin in general, and often for particular sins. "Why doth a living man complain; a man for the punishment of his sin?" How light is this correction, when it is compared with what we deserve? If this, joined to the other sorrows of life, be all the chastisement we are to receive, for our ingratitude and numerous offences, how cheerfully should it be endured; especially when the great recompense, at last, is contemplated ?—Our afflictions, or our works, how grievous or how great soever they may be, cannot, indeed, be a satisfaction for sin, and the ground of our acceptance by Heaven. These transcendent blessings are derived to us from an infinitely higher source, the sacrifice and merits of the Redeemer of the world, through the medium of our faith. But works that are truly good, are not to be undervalued. They are the genuine fruits and evidences of true faith; they are acceptable to the God of love and mercy; and they are required by him, as our indispensable duties.

These views of Divine Providence and Grace, if they were thoroughly impressed on our minds, would have a strong tendency to reconcile us, not only to bodily afflictions, but to all the distresses and trials, which the wisdom and goodness of our heavenly Father may be pleased to appoint for us.

I was often solicited to compose and publish a Grammar of the English language, for the use of some teachers, who were not perfectly satisfied with any of the existing grammars. I declined, for a considerable time, complying with this request, from a consciousness of my inability to do the subject that justice, which would be expected in a new publication of this nature. But being much pressed to undertake the work, I, at length, turned my attention seriously to it. I conceived that a grammar containing a careful selection of the most useful matter, and an adaptation of it to the understanding, and the gradual progress, of learners, with a special regard to the propriety and purity of all the examples and illustrations; would be some improvement on the English grammars which had fallen under my notice. With this impression, I ventured to produce the first edition of a work on this subject. It appeared in the spring of the year 1795. I will not assert, that I have accomplished all that I proposed. But the approbation and the sale which the book obtained, have given me some reason to believe, that I have not altogether failed in my endeavours to elucidate the subject, and to facilitate the labours of both teachers and learners of English grammar.

In a short time after the appearance of the work, a second edition was called for. This unexpected demand, induced me to revise and enlarge the book. It soon obtained an extensive circulation. And the repeated editions through which it passed in a few years, encouraged me, at length, to improve and extend it still further; and, in particular, to support, by some critical discussions, the principles upon which many of its positions are founded.

Soon after the Grammar had been published, I was persuaded to compose a volume of Exercises, calculated to correspond with, and illustrate, by copious examples, all the rules of the Grammar, both principal and subordinate. At the same time, I formed a Key to the Exercises, designed for the convenience of teachers ; and for the use of young persons, who had left school, and who might be desirous, at their leisure, to improve themselves in grammatical studies, and perspicuous composition. In forming these two latter volumes, my design was, not only to exercise the student's ingenuity, in correcting the sentences ; and to excite him to the study of grammar, by the pleasure of feeling his own powers and progress : but to introduce, for his imitation, a great number of sentences, selected from the best writers, and distinguished by their perspicuity and elegance ; and to imbue his mind with sentiments of the highest importance, by interweaving principles of piety and virtue with the study of language. The Exercises and Key were published in 1797 ; and met with a greater sale than I could have supposed. The approbation they received made ample amends to me, for the time and labour I had bestowed upon them. And I was encouraged, in the same year, to make an Abridgment of the Grammar, for the use of minor schools, and for those who were beginning to study the language. The four volumes being intimately connected, mutually supported and recommended each other. And this circumstance, I believe, induced many teachers to adopt them, in their seminaries of education.

As these books, except the Abridgment, were reprinted at York, I consented to correct the press ; by which, I presume, they appeared with a greater degree of accuracy, (a point of considerable importance to books designed for schools,) than if they had not received the author's inspection. This circumstance contributed to occupy some of my leisure hours ; and, for a time, afforded a little amusement. Inconvenient as the employment afterwards proved, when it increased much beyond my expectation, I still continued it, with a hope that it would be productive of good effects. My examination of the new editions, gave occasion to many corrections and considerable enlargements ; which I flatter myself, have improved the books, and rendered them less unworthy of the extensive patronage which they have received.

In the course of my literary labours, I found that the mental exercise which accompanied them, was not a little beneficial to my health. The motives which excited me to write, and the objects which I hoped to accomplish, were of a nature calculated to cheer the mind, and to give the animal spirits a salutary impulse. I am persuaded, that if I had suffered my time to pass away, with little or no employment, my health would have been still more impaired, my spirits depressed, and perhaps my life considerably shortened. I have, therefore, reason to deem it a happiness, and a source of gratitude to Divine Providence, that I was enabled, under my bodily weakness and confinement, to turn my attention to the subjects which have, for so many years, afforded me abundant occupation. I think it is incumbent upon us, whatever may be our privations, to cast our eyes around, and endeavour to discover, whether there are not some means yet left us, of doing good to ourselves and to others; that our lights may, in some degree, shine in every situation, and, if possible, be extinguished only with our lives. The quantum of good which, under such circumstances, we do, ought not to disturb or affect us. If we perform what we are able to perform, how little soever it may be, it is enough; it will be acceptable in the sight of Him, who knows how to estimate exactly all our actions, by comparing them with our disposition and ability.

These considerations, joined to the unexpected success which I had met with in my publications, encouraged me to persevere in my literary pursuits. I engaged in a work, which appeared to me likely to prove of peculiar advantage to the rising generation. This was a compilation containing some of the most esteemed pieces in the language, both in prose and poetry: which are at once calculated to promote correct reading; to give a taste for justness of thought, and elegance of composition; and to inculcate pious and virtuous sentiments. This work I entitled, "The English Reader": and I was pleased to find that my hopes respecting it, were not disappointed. The book was introduced, as I wished it to be, into many schools and private families; and it has been often reprinted.

The approbation given to the English Reader, induced me to publish an "Introduction" and a "Sequel" to that book. These three volumes pursue the same objects; they all aim at a chaste and guarded education of young persons. And I have great satisfaction in reflecting, that whilst they contain many selections which present the moral virtues, religion, and the Christian religion in particular, in very amiable points of view, not a sentiment has been admitted into any of them, which can pain the most virtuous mind, or give the least offence to the eye or ear of modesty.

The recommendations which these books received, for the chastity and correctness of sentiment, which distinguish the pieces they contain, persuaded me to believe, that a collection, in French, on similar principles, and made from some of the finest writers ; would be received by the public, with some degree of approbation. Animated by this expectation, I produced in the year 1802, a compilation entitled, "Lecteur François" ; and in 1807, another, with the title of "Introduction au Lecteur François". As the contents of both these volumes are extracted from authors of reputation, and are particularly guarded in point of sentiment and morality, I hoped that they would be acceptable to teachers of schools, and private instructers, as well as to the young persons who were under their care, and others who wished to improve themselves in the language. I have had no reason to regret the time and pains, which I employed, in preparing and producing these volumes. In foreign languages, not less than in English, it is of high importance, that youth should be presented with books inculcating sound morality, and purified from every thing, which might stain the delicacy of their minds. And I trust that, in these respects, as well as with regard to purity of style and justness of composition, these volumes will bear the strictest examination.

In the year 1804, I published a Spelling Book. When it first occurred to me to compose this little book, and for some time afterwards, the work appeared to be of so very humble a nature, that I was not in much haste to set about it. On reflecting, however, that a Spelling-book is commonly the threshold of learning; and that, by introducing into it a number of easy reading lessons, calculated to attract attention, the infant mind might be imbued with the love of goodness, and led to approve and practise many duties connected with early life; my hesitation was removed, and, after a considerable time, the work was completed. But I found it much more difficult than I expected. The adaptation of lessons to the young capacity, and the exactness required in the gradations of instruction, appeared to demand all the judgment and attention of which I was master; and probably called for much more than I possessed. After many essays, I came at length to the end of my labour. I made it a point, in composing the Spelling-Book, to introduce no matter that is foreign to the objects, which such a work ought to have in view; and I was studious to bring the latter reading lessons to such a state of advancement, as would form an easy and a natural connexion between this book and the "Introduction to the English Reader."

From the friend whom I am now addressing, and at whose request these Memoirs are written, I certainly received much valuable, and very material, assistance, in compiling the Spelling-Book, "The Introduction to the English Reader," and the two volumes in French: and I cannot, with propriety, omit, on the present occasion, the acknowledgment of this co-operation. It is also proper to add, in this place, that I received from the same hand, and from a number of my literary correspondents, many very useful suggestions and criticisms, with respect to my English Grammar, and some of my other publications. These hints and criticisms have undoubtedly contributed, in no small degree, to improve the books, and to render them less unworthy of the attention which they have received from the public.

As I was desirous that my publications should have a circulation as extensive as I could procure for them, I sold the copyrights to one of the first houses in London. These booksellers had it in their power to spread them very diffusively; and they have done it perfectly to my satisfaction. They gave a liberal price for the books: and I must say, that in all our transactions together, which have not been very limited, they have demonstrated great honour and uprightness, and entirely justified my confidence and expectations. I have great pleasure in knowing that the purchase of the copyrights has proved highly advantageous to them: and though it has turned out much more lucrative, than was at first contemplated, they are fully entitled to the benefit. Such contracts always have in them some degree of hazard; and it was possible that these might have been attended with little or no profit.

But my views in writing and publishing were not of a pecuniary nature. My great objects were, as I before observed, to be instrumental in doing a little good to others, to youth in particular; and to give my mind a rational and salutary employment. It was, I believe, my early determination, that if any profits should arise from my literary labours, I would apply them not to my own private use, but to charitable purposes, and for the benefit of others. My income was sufficient to support the expenses of my family, and to allow of a little to spare; and I had not any children to provide for. There was consequently no inducement to warrant me, in deviating from the determination I had made: and as I have hitherto adhered, I trust I shall continue faithfully to adhere, to my original views and intentions. By these observations, I do not design any censure on those writers, who apply the profits of their works, to increase the amount of their property. Many persons, from their situation, their connexions, and other considerations, find this application proper or necessary. Every case must be decided by its own peculiar circumstances: and whilst we claim indulgence to our own sentiments and conduct, we should be liberally disposed to make every allowance for those who think and act differently.

After the Grammar and the books connected with it, had passed through many editions, the proprietors conceived that an edition of the whole, in two volumes octavo, on fine paper, and in a large letter, would be well received by the public; and I embraced the opportunity, to improve the work, by many additions which I conceived to be appropriate. These occupied about one hundred pages of the first volume. In its present form, the publication is designed for the use of persons, who may think it merits a place in their libraries. To this privilege it may, perhaps, be allowed to aspire, as a work containing a pretty extensive exhibition of the principles of English grammar, and a copious illustration of those principles; with the addition of some positions and discussions, which I persuade myself are not destitute of originality. It will, therefore, I venture to hope, serve as a book of reference, to refresh the memory, and, in some degree, to employ the curiosity of persons who are skilled in grammar, as well as to extend the knowledge of those who wish to improve themselves in the art. This octavo edition of the Grammar appeared in 1808. It was favourably received; and a new edition of it was ordered in the course of a few months.

At this period, I had the satisfaction to perceive, that all my literary productions were approved; and that most of them were advancing in the public estimation. But I was fully persuaded, that an author ought to terminate his labours, before the tide of favour begins to turn; and before he incurs the charge of being so infected with the morbid humour for writing, as not to have the discretion to know when to stop. I was so sensible of what was due to the public, for their favourable reception of my productions, that I was extremely unwilling to forfeit their approbation, by presuming too much on what I had experienced. It appears to be better to retire from the field of public labour, with some advantages, than to incur the risk of losing all, or of impairing what has been acquired, by feeble and unsuccessful efforts to obtain more. I may add to these observations, that I had, perhaps, pursued this mode of employment rather too closely; and that I wished for more leisure to prosecute other studies. Influenced by these various motives, I have closed my literary labours, for the present at least; and I shall not resume them, unless some special considerations should alter my views of the subject. There will, I trust, still remain for me, other sources of employment, and some degree of usefulness, better adapted to circumstances, and to my growing infirmities of body.

It may not be improper for me, on this occasion, to express the comfortable hope which I entertain, that, notwithstanding my infirmities and privations, I have been an instrument of some good to others, by my studies and publications. This is a source of grateful acknowledgment to the Giver of all good, and Disposer of all events. But I must not be misunderstood. I arrogate nothing to myself: I have nothing to boast of. If I have done any thing that is acceptable to God, it has been but little; and that little has been produced by his gracious assistance, and accepted for the sake of Jesus Christ. In reflecting on my errors and transgressions through life, my numberless omissions of what I ought to have done, and commissions of what I ought not to have done, I perceive abundant cause for deep humiliation; and for esteeming very lightly, and exceedingly defective, my endeavours to promote the interests of virtue, and to do the will of my heavenly Father.

I have occasionally, in these Memoirs, made some observations on the importance of learning and knowledge to the human mind: but it may not be improper to express my sentiments more explicitly, on this interesting subject.—I consider these attainments, as of so great consequence to us, in civil, moral, and religious points of view, that it would be difficult to calculate the benefits which they produce. And yet, like most, if not all other, advantages, they may be overvalued, misapplied, or pursued to excess. This is unhappily the case, when they nourish pride and vanity; occupy too much of our time; or interfere with the great duties of loving and serving our Creator, and promoting the welfare, spiritual or temporal, of our fellow-creatures. All our duties of every kind, all the rational and allowable concerns of life, are perfectly consistent, and harmonize together, when they are pursued according to their respective importance, and in due subordination to one another. If, therefore, in the acquisition of learning and knowledge, and in the enjoyments which they afford us, we perceive that the supreme love of God prevails in our hearts; that the interest and happiness of others are warmly and properly felt; and that our own wellbeing hereafter, is the chief aim and concern of our lives; we may securely trust, that our studies and literary engagements, are not only innocent and allowable, but conducive to the great ends of our existence. These, indeed, appear to be the true tests, by which we may ascertain the rectitude of all our views and pursuits.

In the prosecution of classical learning, not only the limitations and tendencies just mentioned, are to be regarded, but particular caution and restraint are requisite, especially in the education of young persons. It will doubtless be admitted, that several of the ancient celebrated authors contain passages which, in point of religion, morality, and even decency, are very exceptionable; that they have a strong tendency to corrupt the tender minds of youth; and to leave impressions which, in mature years, may foster their depravities, or, at least, increase the conflicts of virtue.

There are, indeed, some editions of the classics, which have received a considerable degree of purgation; for which the world is not a little indebted to the worthy labourers, in this department of literature.* But there is, perhaps, much yet remaining, in several of them, which calls for the purifying operations of some judicious, learned, and conscientious persons. And till this complete purification takes place, I conceive it is of high importance, that a scrupulously selected number of these ancient works should be adopted, not in a few only, but in all our classical seminaries.

---

* A purified edition of the British Poets, was also an object which Mr. Murray had much at heart. Editor.

This selection would doubtless exclude some books, which are distinguished by the simplicity and elegance of their style, and the correctness of their composition. But this sacrifice would be of little moment, compared with the great benefits which it would produce. Fine language and beautiful composition prove the more dangerous, when they are the vehicles of corrupt and pernicious sentiments. They certainly can never compensate for the wounds to virtue, which they serve so deeply, and so often permanently, to inflict. The exclusion of the objectionable books above alluded to, would be of less consequence, and the less to be regretted, because there would still remain a considerable number and variety of ancient authors, in prose and verse, abundantly sufficient for the classical education of young persons.

After all the care that can be taken, in selecting the best and most purified of those celebrated writers, there will still be found amongst them, great defects in the religion and morality which they inculcate. Much imperfection may remain even where positive vice is excluded. It would, therefore, be of singular advantage to the youthful mind, if teachers would, on all proper occasions, remark to their pupils these imperfections; and contrast them with the pure and perfect principles of the Christian religion. The necessity and importance of Christianity to mankind, and many of its distinguishing doctrines and precepts, would, by this means, be evinced and unfolded to young persons. And it may be reasonably presumed that, in numerous instances, this procedure would not only make the happiest impressions on their susceptible minds, but prepare them for an attachment to our holy religion, which no sophistry or scorn of the infidel, no intercourse with the world, would ever be able to destroy.—I have no doubt that the practice I am recommending, is approved and observed, by many instructers of youth. But it is highly desirable, that a practice so eminently useful, should be universally adopted by classical teachers, both public and private, as an indispensable part of education.

At the close of the year 1808, I met with a most affecting event, in the death of my youngest sister, the wife of Gilbert Colden Willett. She had been, for nearly a year, much indisposed; and the disorder made a gradual progress, till it put a period to her mortal existence, in the forty-fifth year of her age. From the letters of my relations, which mention her decease, and the circumstances attending it, I have derived great consolation. She was so patient, so fully resigned to the will of God, and so well prepared to leave the world, and enter into a state of blessedness; that we have no cause to mourn on her account. She has, doubtless, commenced that life, which is free from temptation and sorrow; and in which she will be unspeakably happy for ever. I rejoice that I have had such a sister; and I trust that the recollection of her pious and bright example, will prove, through life, a source of thankfulness, and an additional incentive to virtue. As I feel so deeply interested in this event, I think that an account of some of her expressions, and her deportment, at and near the closing scene, will not be deemed unsuitable to a narrative which relates the chief occurrences of my life.—For several weeks before her death, she was at times affected with exquisite bodily pain, and was often nearly suffocated by the disorder of her lungs. But her own distresses, which were borne with great patience, did not prevent her from attending to the feelings and situation of her husband and children, her relations and friends. She was solicitous to diminish their care, and to relieve their anxiety about her, as much as possible.

Though her hope and trust in the mercy of God, through Jesus Christ, were strong and unshaken, yet she was very humble, and thought but little of her own attainments. To a person who expressed a desire to take pattern after her, she meekly replied: "I desire to take pattern after the Lord Jesus Christ." In one of her intervals of relief from great pain, a person in the room calling her blessed, she answered: "Not yet blessed." And to her husband who said, he was sure she was going to be happy, she replied: "Not sure, my love; we cannot be sure: but I trust in the mercy of the Almighty." At another time, her husband speaking of her goodness, as the ground of a lively hope, she put her hand on his lips, as if to silence him on the subject of herself. On observing the grief of her sister, at a particular time, she said to her: "I hope there is no cause for grief:" and, on another occasion, when her sister was much distressed with beholding her extreme agony of body, she lifted up her finger, with a view to recommend to her submission to the will of God.

Perceiving her husband to be in great affliction, she said to him: "Remember who it is that inflicts the blow. It is intended for your good; and, I trust, for mine." At one time, just after she had recovered from great difficulty in breathing, she said to her friends who were near her: "Fix your heart upon God, and he will support you in an hour like this. Be good, and you will be happy." To one of her domestics, she addressed herself thus: "Farewell, my dear Jane. Remember my advice. If I am happy, you may be so too. You have, I believe, a good heart. May God Almighty bless you!"

With great composure, she gave her husband particular directions respecting her funeral: and, at the same time, desired him to communicate her love to her absent relations, mentioning most of them by their names. She expressed a tender concern, that these observations might not afflict him; and said, that she should not be taken away the sooner, for having made them. It appeared, through the whole of her deportment, that though her heart and views were directed towards heaven, she did not forget the duties that remained to be performed upon earth. She thanked her husband, in the most affectionate manner, for his attentions to her; and expressed regret that he had suffered so much confinement. With a countenance unusually expressive, she said to him: "My beloved husband, I believe I have been favoured with the sweet spirit of my blessed Saviour. O, the comfort and consolation afforded to my soul! He will support me on this trying occasion. Look to him, my dear: he will sustain you; and enable you to be an example to our dear children. O, that you, and they, and all my relations and friends, may feel that pleasing hope, which will support you during life! You must patiently acquiesce in the Divine will. I have, for many years, been a poor, feeble woman: but now, my strength and hope are great in Him who gave, and in Him who taketh away; blessed be his holy name!"

The day preceding her death, she put up a prayer to her heavenly Father, beseeching him, in a sweet and melodious voice, that he would be pleased to bless her beloved husband, her dear sisters, and her lovely and loving children; saying, that he could take much better care of them than she was able to do.

The same day, whilst she was supported to sit up in bed, she expressed a desire to see her children, and to speak to them. They came to her; and kneeled down at her bed side, that they might the more reverently attend to the expressions of their dying mother. This was a most affecting scene, which totally overcame her husband, who was taken out of the room. Her weakness of body was so great, that she was just able to give them her last blessing, and to take leave of them, individually, in these expressive words: "Farewell, my beloved!"—To her other relations and friends who were present, she gave her hand with the utmost composure, as a token of her love, and final separation from them in this world.

The awful period was now approaching, in which her spirit was to sustain its last conflict.

When she was near her end, and in great distress of body, she still felt for the sorrows of her husband; and fearing that the scene would too much affect him, she waved her hand, as a signal for him to leave the room. In about half an hour after this, her pains abated; and she calmly breathed her last, without sigh or groan, uttering these consoling words, expressive of her piety and faith: "Sweet Jesus, take me to thyself!"

Thus terminated the life of this good and pious sister; who exchanged, I doubt not, the sorrows of time for the joys of eternity. Though her trials and afflictions were great, yet compared with the happiness she now enjoys, and which she will for endless ages enjoy, they are lighter than can be conceived; and deserve no consideration but that which is derived from their salutary effects. I have reason to believe, that she found the troubles and disappointments of this life, a great incitement to piety and virtue; a powerful motive to look for that felicity in a better world, which she perceived was not to be met with in this. One source of perpetual gratitude and praises to her gracious Benefactor, will doubtless be, the afflictions which his good Providence saw meet to dispense, in order to wean her from too great an attachment to the things of this life. When we view afflictions in this light, they almost lose their nature; and dispose us to receive them as friendly visiters, as blessings in disguise.

I have, at length, after many delays and interruptions, brought the Memoirs of my life to the present period, the spring of the year 1809; and I hope I shall be able to finish the work, in my next letter.

I am, with much respect and regard, &c.

LETTER VI.

My dear Friend,

I SHALL close the account which I had undertaken to give of the chief events of my life, with a few reflections and observations, which naturally arise on the review of scenes and transactions that so intimately concern me.

I have often deeply regretted, and, if memory last, I shall often regret through life, that a great part of my time has been spent, in too earnest a pursuit of the enjoyments of this transient scene, and in little attention to the interests of a life that is infinitely better. I always approved of that wisdom, which provides for a distant and permanent happiness, especially an eternal happiness, though to obtain it many sacrifices of temporary pleasures are to be made; and I was fully persuaded, that a course of piety and virtue, notwithstanding the trials which attend it, is productive of more solid satisfaction, than all the enjoyments with which the most prosperous worldly pursuits are accompanied. I knew that the consciousness of doing well, the approbation of Heaven, and the well grounded hope of future felicity, are sufficient to raise the mind above all the troubles of time, and to give it a dignity and peace, which nothing earthly can confer. But the busy scenes, and the allurements of the world, were before me, and attracting my attention. The animation produced by flattering prospects; an undue solicitude for the approbation of others; the example of numbers around me, in the earnest pursuit of honours, riches, or pleasures; and the expectation that a more convenient season would arrive, for a truly self-denying and serious course of life; all concurred to insnare my heart, and to induce me to postpone, or to pursue irresolutely, those objects which I hoped would, some time or other, form my greatest concern. I did not properly reflect, as I ought to have done, that, besides losing, through these unhappy delays, a great deal of true and solid enjoyment, I rendered the paths of religion more difficult, by strengthening the habits of folly and procrastination; and laid up for myself a store of afflictive recollections during life.

Time thus misemployed could not, however, be recalled: and it was deeply incumbent upon me, to occupy that which remained, in a very different manner; in gratitude, love, and obedience, to my gracious Preserver and Benefactor.—How happy would it be for us, if we were accustomed, in early life especially, to reflect on the nature of sinful indulgences, and their bitter fruits! We should then be disposed, often and earnestly, to pray to God for preservation; and we should escape many gloomy and sorrowful retrospects. There are periods of our lives, when the sins of youth, as well as those of more advanced years, appear with all their peculiar aggravations, and sometimes occasion great dejection and perplexity of mind. Though they may seem to sleep for a while, they will assuredly, at some time, or other, rise up, and trouble our repose. These are urgent motives to resist the temptations to evil, and to prevent the distressing reflections by which it is followed.

But though the violations of duty, and the sense of our demerits, are productive of such uneasy retrospects; and often induce us, emphatically, to say, as the patriarch Jacob did, in a time of great perplexity and trouble; "I am not worthy of the least of all thy mercies;" yet we are not to despond, under this discouraging view of our condition : a gracious remedy is provided, for all these regrets and distresses. To those who truly repent, and believe in Jesus Christ, the Redeemer of the world, a comfortable hope is afforded, that, through his atonement and intercession, their heavenly Father will pardon all their sins; prepare them, by the operations of his Holy Spirit, for an admittance into his blessed kingdom; and animate them with gratitude, love, and praises to him, both now and for ever.

It is scarcely necessary to observe, that whilst I condemn myself, for rating too highly, and pursuing too ardently, the good things of this life, I do not mean to insinuate, that they cannot be innocently enjoyed, or that they are to be undervalued by those whose hearts are fixed on a better world. We sometimes, however, meet with persons of a serious and peculiar cast of mind, who declaim against the enjoyments of life, not only as things of short duration; but as vanities which are not worth our attention, and above which the pious man is so far elevated, as to look down upon them with contempt. This is a sentiment which, I think, ought not, on any occasion, to be indulged. The follies and vanities of life, are, indeed, to be despised; and they are despised, by those who are truly good. But the provision which Divine Providence has graciously made, for our accommodation and comfort as we pass through this world, demands the attention of a wise and religious man; and it should be received with gratitude to the Giver of every good gift. How elevated soever his mind may be above this transient scene, he contemplates its lawful enjoyments as happily suited to his present state of existence; and he partakes of them with a cheerful and thankful heart. On this subject, the devout Addison has beautifully and gratefully expressed his sentiments.

Ten thousand thousand precious gifts,
My daily thanks employ;
Nor is the least a cheerful heart,
That tastes those gifts with joy.

Through ev'ry period of my life,
Thy goodness I'll pursue;
And after death, in distant worlds,
The glorious theme renew.

At the same time that the pious and grateful man perceives, that to him belongs "the promise of the life that now is," as well as "of that which is to come," he is deeply sensible of the danger and temptations to which he is exposed; and he feels it his duty to keep a perpetual watch, lest the continual and urgent solicitation of the pleasant things around him, should draw away his heart from the love of God, and a proper concern for his future happiness. He is anxious to set a due and proportionate value on all the Divine gifts, spiritual and temporal. I can conceive of no higher wisdom, or greater enjoyment on earth, than this grateful sense of Divine bounty; this due subordination of earthly to heavenly blessings; joined to a steady reliance on the goodness and mercy of God, for his protection through this life, and an inheritance in his blessed kingdom for ever. Compared with these pious and rational enjoyments, all the vain pleasures of a worldly life, spent in forgetfulness of our great Benefactor, are, indeed, light as air, and empty as the bubbles of the deep.

With regard to the privations and trials, with which it has pleased Divine Providence to visit me, I hope I may say, without assuming too much to myself, that I have long acquiesced in my lot, with resignation and cheerfulness. Though I have had, for more than twenty years, great debility of body, and almost constant confinement, proceeding from my inability to walk, I do not recollect that, in the course of this trying period, I ever repined at my situation, or expressed a dissatisfied sentiment respecting it, except on one occasion. This happened in the first year of my indisposition, and was produced by the following circumstance. I had made considerable efforts to overcome the disorder with which I was affected. But perceiving no good effect from any of them, I began to be tolerably reconciled to my condition. At this time, another physician was called in, to assist the family doctor; and by his earnest recommendation, I was induced to take a particular medicine, from which he and myself anticipated much benefit. But instead of being useful, it proved injurious to me. The sanguine hope of relief which I had indulged, made me feel the disappointment very severely: and contemplating, at that moment, my prime of life, and the prosperous circumstances with which I was surrounded, I foolishly said, it was hard that I should be deprived of health, at a time when it appeared to be so peculiarly desirable. This expression was scarcely uttered, when my heart condemned me for its rashness. I felt remorse for this want of submission to Divine Providence; and was much humbled under the sense of my folly. The painful reflections which I had, on this occasion, probably contributed to make me more guarded, in future, against the admission of thoughts so unjust and irreverent. There has, indeed, amidst all my privations, been no cause for murmuring. I have possessed so many comforts, so many sources of real enjoyment, that I have often thought my debility and confinement could scarcely be called an affliction. And I sincerely lament, that I have so little improved the blessings which have been conferred upon me.

When I contemplate my own unworthiness, and the goodness of God to me, through the whole course of my life, I feel that I cannot be too humble, nor too grateful for his manifold mercies. I cannot, indeed, be sufficiently thankful for them. Amidst the numerous blessings which I have received, it has afforded me peculiar satisfaction, that I have been disposed to ascribe them all to Him, as the Origin and Giver of every thing that is good; as the Parent, Redeemer, and Sanctifier, of men. If I consider him as my Creator and Preserver; as the Author of the laws and operations of nature; as the Controller and Director of these laws and operations; as the immediate Bestower of benefits; or, as our Deliverer from sin and misery, and our hope of eternal life, through the sacrifice and merits of his beloved Son, the Lord Jesus Christ: I perceive that he is the Source whence every blessing is derived, and the great Object of gratitude and love. But as this is a subject of high importance, and on which I love to dwell, my friend will not, I am sure, think it improper, if I express myself upon it with more particularity.

As my Creator and Preserver, I owe to him all the faculties of my soul and body, all the capacities which I have for the enjoyment of corporeal, intellectual, and spiritual objects; and, consequently, all the advantage and pleasure that I have received from these sources.

As the Author of the laws of nature, of the material, animal, and rational world, I am indebted to him for every benefit, which I have derived from this grand system of Divine wisdom and goodness. He has not only given me powers to receive happy impressions, but he has arranged and disposed his works, so that their regular operations supply those powers with objects, which are calculated to employ and gratify them. When this great machine of nature, or any part of it, produces in me pleasurable or beneficial effects, I must attribute them all to its beneficent Author, who superintends and permits these operations. If I am, at any time, enabled to conduct myself so happily, as to receive particular benefits from this arrangement and operation of second causes, I still owe them all to Him, who has both presented the feast, and given me power to partake of it, and liberty to choose what is best for me. If, therefore, I am tempted to ascribe any thing exclusively to myself, from the right use of my ability, as a free agent, I am instantly checked by the reflection, that this ability itself is the gift of God.

I cannot, on this occasion, avoid making a few observations, respecting this important sentiment, the free agency of man. Whatever difficulties attend the subject, and how perplexed soever it may have been rendered, by the reasonings of subtle and ingenious disputants ; I never had a doubt of its existence. The consciousness which we have of such a power in the human mind, and the necessity there is for it, in order to make us accountable beings ; the correspondent declarations of the Holy Scriptures, and the dealings of God with men, which always suppose them to be free moral agents ; afford such evidence of the truth of this fundamental article of religion, as appears to me irresistible. If we are unable rationally to explain this principle of action, and to reconcile it with other great truths ; we should reflect, that our intellectual powers are of a very limited nature ; that there are many things which we do not understand, but which we firmly believe ; some points of doctrine which we must admit, without being, at present, able to explain them. That profound philosopher, the venerable Locke, entertained the most unshaken belief, both in the prescience of the Divine Being, and in the free agency of man; though he confessed that his finite capacity was not able to reconcile them.—When we have sufficient evidence for truths which we cannot clearly comprehend, and humbly submit to that evidence, faith becomes a special virtue, and weakness is converted into strength.—I will not pursue this subject any further, but proceed in my remarks on the benefits we receive, and in tracing the great Object of our gratitude.

As the Controller and Director of the laws of nature, I am under peculiar obligations to him, for all the comforts and benefits, which, in consequence of this direction, I have received. This divine interposition to overrule, and appoint the operation of second causes, natural and moral, and make them answer his sovereign purposes, constitutes the special government and providence of God. And all the good obtained, and evil avoided, from this interposition, must be attributed to Him, who not only superintends, but rules and directs, all things, according to his pleasure; who can turn aside impending calamities, and convert that into good, which, in its natural progress or design, would have been productive of injury to us.

If I consider the Divine Being, as immediately influencing my mind, by the operation of his Holy Spirit; consoling me under affliction; guarding me in prosperity; strengthening my faith; animating me to piety and virtue, and supporting me in temptation: I perceive that he is eminently entitled to my gratitude and praise, for all the blessings which I receive by these gracious communications. He has access to the human mind, and knows all its wants and imperfections; and he has promised to give the Holy Spirit, to be a light and defence, a support and comfort, to those who implore his assistance, and put their trust in the Divine Redeemer of the world. And most assuredly he does not fail to perform these sacred promises to the children of men, though the mode of his communications is incomprehensible.

I consider myself as under deep obligations to God, for the trials and afflictions with which he has been pleased to visit me, as well as for the prosperous events of my life. They have been the corrections and restraints of a wise and merciful Father; and may justly be ranked among the number of my choicest blessings. I am firmly persuaded, that cross occurrences, and adverse situations, may be improved by us to the happiest purposes. The spirit of resignation to the will of Heaven, which they inculcate, and the virtuous exertions to which they prompt us, in

order to make the best of our condition, not only often greatly amend it, but confer on the mind a strength and elevation, which dispose it to survey with less attachment the transient things of time, and to desire more earnestly the eternal happiness of another world.

I must not omit to mention, on this occasion, that I consider it as a distinguished felicity, demanding the most grateful acknowledgments to Almighty God, that I have lived in a part of the world, which has been enlightened by the rays of the Gospel; where the Holy Scriptures, in their genuine purity and excellence, are read and understood; and where many bright examples of piety and virtue, in the various ranks and walks of life, demonstrate the divine efficacy of the sublime truths and precepts of Christianity. This is a blessing which it is difficult fully to appreciate. A survey of the condition of those nations, in point of religion and morality, on whom the light of the Gospel has not yet shone, may afford us some conception of our inestimable privilege, in possessing this Sacred Volume: which, as an excellent writer * observes, "has God for its author; salvation for its end; and truth, without any mixture of error, for its matter."

* Locke.

From the preceding enumeration and view of these most interesting subjects, even in so concise and imperfect a manner, it must be evident, that all our benefits, by whatever means they are conveyed to us, are derived from God, the Fountain of life and goodness. And it is scarcely possible to contemplate the blessings, which have been so abundantly bestowed upon us; and to reflect on our own unworthiness; without being deeply sensible of these mercies, and rendering to our Divine Benefactor the tribute of thanksgiving and praise. On this occasion, the example and devotional spirit of the sweet Psalmist of Israel, naturally present themselves to our minds. He was often and strongly impressed with sentiments of this nature: particularly when he composed the one hundred and third Psalm; in which he thus pours forth his grateful emotions. " Bless the Lord, O my soul! and all that is within me, bless his holy name. Bless the Lord, O my soul! and forget not all his benefits: who forgiveth all thine iniquities: who healeth all thine infirmities: who redeemeth thy life from destruction; and crowneth thee with loving kindness and tender mercies." This devout prince was ever ready to ascribe all the blessings of his life to the goodness of God; and took great delight in recounting his favours, and acknowled-

ging his care and protection. These duties apply to us also; and they are enforced by the most important and interesting considerations.

When we reflect on the universal presence of the Deity, his perfect knowledge of all things, and his gracious declaration, that we are so much regarded by him, that the very hairs of our head are numbered; can we have the least hesitation in acknowledging his goodness, and his most particular providence? his continual, watchful attention over us, and all our concerns, in order to promote our comfort here, and to train us up for happiness hereafter? Should not the knowledge of his sacred presence and guardianship, excite us also to the utmost circumspection, in our thoughts, words, and actions? Have we not abundant encouragement, in all our spiritual and temporal exigencies, to apply to him, with filial confidence, for the aid of his Holy Spirit, to enlighten, relieve, and support us? Surrounded as we are with danger and temptations, and exposed to the assaults of subtle and powerful enemies, how consoling and animating is the thought, that the Lord of heaven and earth knows perfectly our situation; perceives with complacency every virtuous conflict; and graciously interests himself, as a Father and Friend, in our protection and deliverance!—If we were duly influenced by these devout sentiments, we should be prepared for all the vicissitudes of this mutable world; and we should steadily pursue our journey through it, always thankful, and often rejoicing.

In the course of this narrative, I have occasionally made a number of observations on serious and religious subjects; and they are the deliberate convictions of my understanding, and the genuine feelings of my heart. But I must not be understood, as at all intimating, that I have attained the virtues, the objects to which many of these observations refer. I know that I am, indeed, very far from such an attainment; that I have great weaknesses, and many imperfections; and that they are all, in some degree, under the influence of a subtle and powerful adversary, ever watchful to circumvent and destroy. I lament their operation and effects: but I trust that, by Divine Grace, through Jesus Christ, I am, and I shall be, enabled to maintain the warfare against them: and a hope lives in my heart, that, for his sake, I shall finally be made victorious over all my spiritual enemies.

I cannot finish these Memoirs of my life, without expressing, still more particularly, my sense of the greatest blessing which was ever conferred on mankind. I mean, the redemption from sin, and the attainment of a happy immortality, by the atonement and intercession of our Lord and Saviour, Jesus Christ. I contemplate this wonderful proof of the love of God to man, as an act of mercy and benignity, which will stimulate the gratitude and love, the obedience, praise, and adoration, of the redeemed, through ages that will never end. This high dispensation is, in every respect, adapted to our condition, as frail and sinful creatures. In surveying our offences and imperfections, it prevents despondence; directs us where to look for relief; and freely offers us, if we are truly penitent, and believe in Christ, pardon and peace: in reflecting on our religious attainments, it checks presumption, and keeps us humble: and, amidst all the trials and troubles of life, it cheers us with the prospect of a merciful deliverance, and of being soon received into those blissful regions, where we shall be secured, eternally secured, from sin and sorrow; where we shall be admitted into the Divine presence, and unceasingly celebrate, in joyful anthems, the praises of the Father, the Son, and the Holy Spirit, one God blessed for ever. To them who obtain this glorious and happy state, all the afflictions of the longest and most painful life, will then appear to have been, indeed, light and momentary; as a drop of the ocean, as a grain of sand on the seashore, compared with the greatness of their felicity, and the endless ages of its continuance.—That this inestimable blessing, my dear friend, may be ours, when we have quitted this transient scene, is my very fervent desire.

Lindley Murray.

MEMOIRS CONTINUED.

MEMOIRS CONTINUED.

CHAPTER I.

CONCLUDING YEARS OF THE AUTHOR'S LIFE.

I HAVE now presented to the reader the short but interesting recollections of the life of Mr. Murray; which he was induced to write in consequence of my urgent request. They were finished in the spring of 1809; and committed to my care in the autumn of that year. On me devolves the task of completing them. Not long before the author's decease, as well as at other times, I wished and earnestly desired him, to bring them down to a much later period: which, I believe, he would have done if his life had been prolonged. The addition would, I doubt not, have been peculiarly interesting and edifying; and would perhaps have afforded an almost unequalled proof of vigour of mind, and warmth of benevolent and devotional feeling, in very advanced age. But as he has performed more than I originally either proposed or expected, I have no cause to complain; and nothing to lament, but my inability to do justice to the subject. A short account of the concluding years of his life, his character, and some remarks on his publications, will, I apprehend, comprise all that is requisite for the information of the reader, and will complete my tribute to the memory of this excellent man.

In the course of the narrative, I shall introduce a few circumstances, which, according to the strict order of time, should have been inserted in Mr. Murray's own Memoirs; but which, from modesty, and other obvious motives, he has omitted.

Soon after the conclusion of his Memoirs, he experienced a considerable increase of debility and indisposition; from which he did not think he should recover. In that expectation, he frequently expressed, as on many similar occasions, his assured hope of happiness in the life to come, through the merits and mediation of our blessed Lord Jesus Christ; utterly disclaiming all confidence in any good deeds that he had been enabled to do, and all idea of acceptance with God, through them, or for them.

Till this period, he was able to go out daily

in his carriage; and in summer, he was frequently drawn about his garden in a chair conveniently made for that purpose. But he was at length induced, though reluctantly, to relinquish all the little exercise which he had been accustomed to take. He found that even a very small degree of bodily exertion, increased the muscular weakness of his limbs; and that exposure to the air occasioned frequent and severe colds, together with other indisposition. The last time he went out in his carriage, was in autumn, 1809. From that time till his decease, the space of upwards of sixteen years, he was wholly confined to the house; with the exception of one or two times, when, after an illness, he went out in a sedan, but without receiving any benefit.

The total want of exercise appears to have brought on a painful disorder; which, in June, 1810, terminated in the discharge of a small stone. His sufferings for some days were severe, and, for a few hours, acute: but his mind was, as usual, calm and resigned. In an interval of comparative ease, he said: "My trust is in the mercy of God, through Christ, my Redeemer. Nothing which I have done, that may seem meritorious, affords me any satisfaction, on reflection, except as an earnest of divine mercy and goodness." Having voided the stone, and finding instant relief, he exclaimed, with lively and grateful feeling: "I am eased of my pain! I have great cause to be thankful, even if the relief should prove but temporary."

Some time afterwards he had a slight return of a similar disorder. And for several succeeding years, he was much afflicted with oppressive languor; and with very uncomfortable sensations in his head, stomach, and bowels. But, upon the whole, his health was not so much impaired as might have been expected, from his total confinement to the house, his advanced age, and enfeebled constitution. His spirits were, with very slight exceptions, uniformly good; his demeanour was, at all times, gentle; and his disposition, mild, cheerful, and obliging.

When his health would allow, he found, till the close of life, much useful occupation, and even amusement, in revising and improving his works. His grammatical productions, in particular, engaged a considerable portion of his time and attention. As the public had so liberally approved and encouraged them, he thought it was incumbent upon him, to bring them as near as he could to a state of completeness. He was particularly solicitous to render them explicit, and free from difficulty; to remove objections which had occurred, and to prevent others which might be formed, to different parts of the works. These objects, though important, he has in many instances accomplished, without much alteration. "By the change of a word," he observes, "a slight variation in the form of a phrase, an additional sentence, or a short note, I have, as I think, frequently removed an objection or difficulty, and made that perspicuous, which seemed to be obscure or ambiguous. And I believe that all these variations have been effected, without any material deviations from the original plan and principles of the Grammar."—To the octavo Grammar, he made large and important additions, as well as corrections. The later editions of the duodecimo Grammar, Exercises, and Key, also underwent much amendment. To enlarge and improve the Power of Religion, was, from its first publication to the latest period of the author's life, a favourite object of his attention. But his parental care and regard were bestowed on all his works. Whatever he found erroneous or deficient in one edition, he corrected or supplied in another. The editions pressed close upon him: but they seldom failed to receive from him some portion of attention, and consequent benefit. No author, I believe, ever had so much opportunity to revise, improve, and enlarge his works; and no one could have availed himself of it, with greater judgment, or more unwearied vigilance.

He was induced, also, to prepare some new

publications, which he conceived would be useful. Having himself derived much benefit and satisfaction from the frequent perusal of bishop Horne's Commentary on the Psalms, and being desirous of extending that benefit to others, he made and published "A Selection" from that invaluable work. It was well received; and has been approved and recommended by several very respectable public critics.

He wrote also a little piece, published in 1817, "On the Duty and Benefit of a daily Perusal of the Holy Scriptures." It is well composed; and, I doubt not, it has promoted, in no small degree, the important object which the author had in view. It expresses, in striking terms, the reverence which he felt for the Scriptures; and the benefit which he derived from that serious perusal of them, which he recommends to others. To endeavour reverently to compose the mind, before any portion of Scripture is read or heard; and when it is finished, to allow time, by a short pause, for devout meditation, or useful reflection, on what has been read or heard; is advice well worthy of attention, and consonant with Mr. Murray's own practice. The inefficacy which usually attends the reading of the Bible, is not owing to any defect in the sacred volume; but to the want of serious attention, or of previous preparation, in those who read or hear.

Mr. Murray, from his retired life and unassuming character, did not receive any of those academical honours, to which the publication of his grammatical works, no doubt, fully entitled him. A tribute of respect was, however, paid to him by two literary societies at New York. In 1810, he was elected an honorary member of the Historical Society; and in 1816, of the Literary and Philosophical Society. But he was not covetous of honour. The high approbation which his works received, was gratifying to him; chiefly because it was an earnest and a proof of their usefulness.

His acquaintance and society, particularly after his works had obtained celebrity, were much courted by respectable and literary persons. But there was a genuine humility, and even a diffidence, in his nature, which seemed to shrink from the idea of personally attracting any share of public curiosity or observation. The general debility under which he laboured, and which was usually increased by the exertion necessarily attendant on the receiving of strangers, and conversing with them, was, however, the chief cause which induced him to decline much company. Indeed, the calls, and applications for introduction, which he received, were so numerous, that had he encouraged them, the early and regular hours which he kept, would have been much broken in upon, and the leisure which he enjoyed for literary pursuits, greatly interrupted: and it was highly desirable that his valuable time should be preserved free from invasion.

But he did not, on any occasion, decline company, because he was unsocial, or, in the slightest degree, hypochondriacal. His friends frequently visited him: they knew the hours most suitable to him; they were careful not to encroach too much on his time; and they did not expect him to converse, when higher engagements, or indisposition, rendered it inconvenient. He took a lively concern in the transactions of his domestic circle; and conversed, with interest, on public affairs. When he was in a tolerable state of health, no one more cheerfully enjoyed, or more agreeably promoted, social intercourse. Far from needing consolation from his visiters, he communicated it to them. Like a gentle stream by the way side, he enlivened and refreshed them.

Many strangers, however, and distinguished literary persons, were at different times, and on various occasions, introduced to him; and expressed, in strong terms, the pleasure which they derived from the interview: amongst these may be particularly mentioned the earl of Buchan, in 1802, and the Edgeworths, in 1803. On the lively fancy of Mr. Edgeworth and his daughter

Maria, their visit to Holdgate formed a very pleasing picture, often reverted to with much satisfaction; in which even "the benevolent looks of Mrs. Murray, when she offered them some cake and wine, were not forgotten." Their visit was in the evening, and wholly unexpected. With the kind reception which they received, they were much gratified. Mr. Murray himself far exceeded their expectation. His personal appearance, his unassuming demeanour, and his conversational powers, excited in their minds a most agreeable surprise. When they called at Holdgate, they were on a tour, of which an excursion to Paris had formed part. Mr. Murray's sequestered little abode, and its happy and respectable inhabitants, formed, no doubt, a very striking contrast to the gay and literary circles in which they had mixed. They considered Mr. and Mrs. Murray as "the most striking example of domestic happiness, and of religion without ostentation, or the spirit of dogmatizing, which they had ever beheld."

Mr. Murray bore his honours so meekly; he was so intelligent, not only on literary subjects, but also on the common affairs of life; and he adapted his conversation, so judiciously and kindly, to the capacities, tastes, and characters, of the persons to whom it was addressed; that no one, whether learned or unlearned, young or old, gay or grave, could partake of it without feeling highly gratified. In him, no one could observe any vanity, egotism, or eccentricity. Few, I believe, ever visited him, who did not hear something from him, to inform their judgment, or to amend their heart.

Seldom did he make his sufferings and privations the subject of conversation. When on any occasion they were mentioned, he never failed to enumerate, and frequently he expatiated very pathetically on, the many alleviating and comfortable circumstances that attended them: the pleasantness of his dwelling; the kindness of his friends; the constant company, and affectionate attention, of his wife; his ability to pursue literary occupations; and the calm state of his mind. He would sometimes say: "When I first lost the use of my limbs, and saw my friends walking about, and pursuing their respective business or amusement, I wished to be, and to do, like them: but now, by long use, confinement has become familiar to me; and, I believe, it is less irksome and afflictive, than many persons, who have not experienced it, would imagine. My blessings far overbalance my afflictions. Indeed, I have so many enjoyments yet left me, and I possess so many comforts, that I can scarcely term my situation an affliction." He often said that what had very much tended to reconcile him to his confinement, was a belief that he had been more extensively useful, than he could have been, if he had continued in the possession of that health and strength which he once enjoyed.

To pass from an author's works to his life and conversation, frequently occasions disappointment: but with respect to Mr. Murray, the transition was honourable. Personal acquaintance increased esteem and regard. Between his life and his works there was a striking coincidence. His writings might be truly called a fair transcript of his mind; and his life and conversation a beautiful exemplification of the moral and religious principles, which his writings uniformly inculcate.

For many years, his infirmities did not allow him to rise from his seat, on the entrance of a visiter; and not unfrequently the weakness of his voice, contracted by severe colds, or by over-exertion, prevented his uttering any words except in a whisper: but on such occasions, his kindly extended hand, and his smile of ineffable benignity, bespoke a welcome far more cordial and affecting, than could have been expressed by any of the usual forms of civility.—When I first saw him, he was forty-eight years of age: but both then, and long afterwards, he looked considerably younger than he really was. The impression which his noble aspect, his gentle demeanour, his cheerful, sensible, and, occasionally, pious conversation, produced on my mind, can never be obliterated whilst my memory continues.

So excellent was his character, so mild and engaging his deportment, that persons having but a very slight acquaintance with him, or seeing him only occasionally on business, seemed to contract a strong personal regard for him: they frequently inquired, with apparent solicitude, respecting his health; and spoke of him in terms of the highest respect and esteem. Even strangers, merely from the report which they heard of him, would solicitously inquire after him; and, not unfrequently, send him some little message, or token, of respect. To know him, though but imperfectly, was to love and esteem him; and if any persons did not love and esteem him, it was because they did not know him, or had not heard the full and true report of his good deeds and amiable disposition.

Mr. Murray was much respected by many of his most distinguished cotemporaries in America. When his works had procured for him a high degree of celebrity, the testimony of their approbation, especially of those with whom he had been personally acquainted, was peculiarly acceptable to him. From his fellow-student, Mr. Jay, and from many other highly respectable persons, he received, on various occasions, letters replete with expressions of esteem, regard, and warm congratulation.

Several of his countrymen, at different times, visited him: two of whom having, in their travels, given an account of their visit, I shall diversify this narrative, by inserting an extract from each.

The first is from "Travels in England, Holland, and Scotland, by Benjamin Silliman, professor of chemistry, at Yale College, Connecticut."

"Towards evening," (Nov. 19, 1805,) "I went out on horseback to Holdgate, a village in the vicinity of York; for the purpose of seeing a countryman of ours, who is well known to the world, both by his writings and the excellence of his character. I carried an introductory letter, which produced me the kindest reception; and all unnecessary ceremony being waved, I was seated at once between Mr. and Mrs. Murray.

Mr. Murray, I need not inform you, enjoys a distinguished literary reputation; and this, although well deserved, is by no means his most enviable distinction, for he is an eminently good man. Being afflicted with a muscular weakness in his limbs, he removed, about twenty years ago, from New York to England, hoping for relief from the temperate climate of this island. The expected benefit he has not been so happy as to obtain; his debility still continues to such a degree, that he can walk only a few steps at once.

I found him sitting on a sofa, to which he has been generally confined for many years. Although unable to benefit mankind by active exertions, in any of the common pursuits of business, he has made full amends by the labours of his mind. In the chaste, perspicuous, and polished style of his writings, in the pure and dignified moral sentiments which they contain, and even in the simple and yet elegant typographical execution, one may discern proofs of the character of the man. He belongs to the society of Friends; but both he and Mrs. Murray have so tempered the strictness of the manners peculiar to their society, that they are polished people, with the advantage of the utmost simplicity of deportment.

I was fortunate in finding Mr. Murray able to converse with freedom; for, at times, he is unable to utter even a whisper, and is compelled to decline seeing his friends. Our conversation related principally to literature, morals, and religion; and the state of these important subjects in the United States and in England. I asked him if he had relinquished the idea of returning to his country, and of observing the great change which these things had undergone in a period of twenty years. He said that he still cherished a faint hope of seeing his native land again; that hope was, like a star, often obscured, but twinkling now and then, to revive his spirits.

One would suppose that a situation so peculiar as that of Mr. Murray, would naturally induce a degree of impatience of temper, or at least of depression of spirits; but I know not that I have ever seen more equanimity, and sweetness of deportment, joined with a more serene and happy cheerfulness, than in this instance. When the painful circumstances of his situation were alluded to, he expressed his gratitude to Heaven, for the many comforts and alleviations which, he said, he enjoyed under his confinement.

You would not judge from his appearance that he is an infirm man, for his countenance is rather ruddy; and it is animated with a strong expression of benevolence. His person is tall, and well-formed; and his manner of conversing is modest, gentle, easy, and persuasive.

Being afraid of inducing him to converse beyond his strength, towards the close of the evening I reluctantly rose to come away; and was solicited, in the most gratifying manner, to protract and repeat my visit. Declining the former, and having no prospect of the latter, I took a cordial farewell of these excellent people; and rode back to York with impressions of the most agreeable kind."

The second extract is from a work entitled, "A Year in Europe, in 1818 and 1819, by John Griscom, professor of chemistry and natural philosophy in the New York Institution."

"Among the social occurrences which I shall remember with the most pleasure, is a visit this afternoon," (27th of February, 1819,) "to our very estimable countryman, Lindley Murray. He still resides at the little village of Holdgate, about three quarters of a mile from the city of York. His increasing infirmity of body has latterly been such, as to prevent him from receiving the visits of strangers. But coming from New York, and being acquainted with his nearest relations, he was induced to yield to my request, and grant me an interview. Though so weak as to be scarcely able to bear his own weight, he has been enabled, by the power of a strong and well balanced mind, and by the exercise of the Christian virtues, to gain a complete ascendancy over himself; and to exhibit an instance of meekness, patience, and humility, which affords, I may truly say, one of the most edifying examples I have ever beheld. His mind is still clear, sound, and discriminating; and he feels the interest of a true philanthropist, in the progress of education, and the general welfare of his fellow-creatures. I have been informed, by persons who were his youthful cotemporaries, that he was possessed by nature of great vivacity of feeling, and passions not less difficult to control, than those which fall to the ordinary lot of humanity. But so effectually have the graces of the Christian surmounted the waywardness of nature, and diffused their benign influence over the whole tenour of his mind, as to produce upon his countenance, a lustre and a sweetness of expression, 'with less of earth in them than heaven.'

The temperature of his room is regulated by the thermometer. A constant care of this kind, joined to temperance in diet, has enabled him to live without exercise; to support a frame of unusual debility; and to prolong to old age, a life of the greatest usefulness to his fellow-creatures. Having brought with him to England a fortune competent to his moderate wants, he has devoted the whole profit of his literary labours, to the promotion of various benevolent institutions, and to other deeds of charity. He has been blessed with a most amiable and intelligent wife; the companion of his early years, and the faithful and sympathizing partner in all that concerns him. A young woman, who serves them as housekeeper, appears also well qualified, by the respectability of her character and acquirements, to perform the duties of an almost filial trust.

It is thirty-four years since this worthy pair left their native shores: but their feelings are still American; and to listen to a particular relation of the enlargement of our cities, and the progress of the country, afforded them evidently the most lively satisfaction; while, at the same time, a consideration of the small number of the numerous acquaintance they left behind, who are now on the stage of life, gave to the conversation a placid melancholy, which served but to increase the warmth and tenderness of the interview."

Mr. Murray lived, during a long course of years, a very retired life. Though an object of general esteem, respect, and admiration, he was known intimately, or even personally, but to few. The following particulars, therefore, respecting his habits and manner of living, though minute, may perhaps be acceptable to the reader, and not devoid of interest; and, in time to come, they may supply the place of vague, traditionary report. In a physical point of view, they may also be useful. It has frequently been made a subject of inquiry, how a person could support entire confinement to the house, and even to one seat, during many years, and yet preserve to the last, a comfortable state

of health, evenness and cheerfulness of spirits, and surprising vigour of mind.

Mr. Murray carefully avoided all habits of indolence, both with respect to body and mind. He generally rose about seven o'clock in the morning; but rather later in the depth of winter. When he was dressed, and seated in an arm chair, which had casters, his wife rolled him, with ease, to the sofa, * in his sitting room; on which, after he gave up taking any exercise, he sat during the whole day. At meal times, the table was brought to him. At other times, a small stand, with a portable writing desk on it, was generally before him. The papers and books which he was using, were laid on the sofa, by his side: but they were usually removed before the entrance of any visiter, as he disliked the parade of literature. His wife sat on a chair close by his side; except when, through courtesy, she relinquished her seat to some friend, or visiter, with whom he wished particularly to converse. The room being rather narrow, the sofa was placed against the wall. Mr. Murray never sat by the fire: but to avoid the draught from the doors and windows, he was obliged to sit nearly opposite; from the ill effects of which, he was guarded by a small

* The sofa which he had brought with him, from America; and on which he sat, or lay, during the voyage.

skreen, between him and the fire. He attributed, in a great measure, the preservation of his sight to extreme old age, to his constantly avoiding the glare of fire and candles. When he read or wrote by candlelight, he used a shade candlestick.

His sitting room was of a good size, and particularly pleasant, having a window at each end: the one with a south aspect, looked to the garden; the other to the turnpike-road, and to some fields, across one of which, was a pathway leading to the city of York. The trees and flowers in his garden, the passengers on the road and pathway, and the rural occupations in the fields, afforded a pleasing diversity of scene, cheering to his mind, and relieving to his eyes, when fatigued with composing, reading, or writing. An awning was placed in summer over the south window, to shade off the rays of the sun. Thus secured, and having a constant but almost imperceptible ventilation, occasioned by two large windows opposite to each other, and also by two doors and the fire, the room was always sweet, fresh, and salubrious. A fire, even in summer, was constantly kept up through the whole day; which, as Mr. Murray justly observed, tended to carry off the noxious particles of air: but the room, in the warmest weather, was considerably cooler and fresher than apartments usually are. Mr. Murray could not bear a partial exposure to the air; therefore, he never sat with the doors or windows open. But in the morning, before he came into the room, it was completely ventilated, by the opening of both windows for a short time; and thus a free current of air was admitted. His bed room was also ventilated, once or twice, during the course of the day. So sensible was he of the pernicious effects of breathing vitiated air, that he never had the curtains of his bed drawn. As a further preventive from over heating his sitting room, he had two of Fahrenheit's thermometers: the one was placed at the outside of the north window; the other was hung in the room, at a distance from the fire. The temperature of the room was usually from sixty-three to sixty-five degrees.

Mr. Murray's bed room was large; it had the same aspect, and was on the same floor, as his sitting room, and opened into it; and had also two windows, one at each end. But as the chimney could not be made to carry up the smoke, he was obliged in all his illnesses, when the weather was cold, to have a bed brought into his sitting room; and in that room, very near the seat on which he had done so much good, he breathed his last, and passed, I trust, from the employments of time to the rewards of eternity.

Soon after he came into his sitting room, in the morning, he took his breakfast; after which, his wife, or some one of his family, read to him a portion of the Scripture, or of some other religious book. Horne's Commentary on the Psalms, and Doddridge's Family Expositor, omitting the notes and paraphrase, were the books which he chiefly used for this purpose, and also for his evening meditation. After a short pause, he proceeded to transact the business of the day, of which the hearing or reading of a daily journal formed part; or he applied immediately to his literary avocations. Until he became wholly confined to the house, he took an airing in his carriage, from twelve till half-past one. At two he dined. After dinner, he sat quite still, closed his eyes, and sometimes dozed, for nearly half an hour; a practice which he brought with him from America, and by which he found his strength and spirits much recruited: then he resumed his occupations; and continued them for some hours, unless interrupted by company. Religious reading in the family, and meditation, closed the day. At ten, he and all his household retired to rest. This course of life he continued, with little variation, during the whole of his residence in England.

There was nothing particular in his diet. It was simple. He did not use tobacco in any shape. He never took spirits, and but seldom wine; and then only half a glass at most. At dinner, he was accustomed, for many years after he came into this country, to take about a gill of London porter: afterwards, he gradually diminished the quantity, until he reduced it only to a wine glass, diluted in warm water. His breakfast and supper were, for some years, new milk, and baked rice, or sometimes toasted bread; latterly, chocolate boiled in milk and water, and bread. At dinner, he partook of meat, vegetables, pudding, and other ordinary dishes; but all cooked in a plain way. He did not, at dinner, eat of more than one dish of meat. In the afternoon, he sometimes took about half a cup of tea, or of milk and water; but more frequently instead of it, a small quantity of strawberries, grapes, or other sweet fruits, out of his garden, or dried plums. Except in serious illness, he took no medicine; and even then but little: being of opinion that the frequent use of it weakens the tone of the stomach. Of the beneficial effects of friction, by the hand simply, he was thoroughly convinced. He made frequent, if not daily use of it; and never failed to have recourse to it when his head, or any part of his body, was affected with uncomfortable sensations, particularly of a rheumatic nature. He was of opinion that it not only produced local benefit; but that, in his particular case, it tended, in a considerable degree, to supply the want of other exercise. His appetite, till within a few years previous to his decease, was good, and rather uncommon, considering his sedentary life. The comfortable state of health and the vigour of mind, which he enjoyed in his old age, must, in a great degree, be ascribed, under the blessing of Providence, to his temperance and moderation, to his judicious self-management, and to that peacefulness and serenity, which are the usual concomitants of a good and pious life.

In the year 1819, Mr. Murray lost his much esteemed brother, John Murray, of New York. This gentleman, in his character, and in some of the circumstances of his life, bore a striking resemblance to our author. He was of a lively and active disposition; kind and generous, humane and pious. Early in life, he engaged in mercantile pursuits, in which he was highly successful: but, in the prime of life, having acquired a competency, he relinquished them, and devoted the remainder of his days to the service of religion and humanity. He was particularly distinguished by his endeavours to promote the abolition of slavery; to ameliorate the condition of the Indians of North America; and to establish and support various institutions at New York, for the relief of poverty, and the improvement of public morals.

He was of a remarkably liberal and catholic spirit. In the prosecution of his benevolent designs, he associated much and freely with persons of various religious denominations. He often expressed an earnest desire, that Christians should avoid unnecessary disputes about non-essentials, and unite in promoting the common cause, in which they all profess to be engaged.

Some years before his death, being at Albany, on public business, when the streets were covered with ice, he had a fall; from the effects of which he never recovered. He continued lame, and in a disabled state of body; and suffered great and almost constant pain: but he endured the affliction with fortitude and Christian patience; nor did it materially interrupt his career of benevolence. He died in an act of supplication to the Lord.—His charities did not terminate with his life. By his last will, he made many ample donations and bequests for public and private benefit. His name is remembered at New York, with respect and gratitude, as a benefactor of his country.

He left behind him two sons, and a widowed daughter: who, in some degree, supplied to Mr. Murray, the loss which he had sustained of a kind and intelligent correspondent, in his native, but far distant land.

After the decease of his brother, our author found himself the last surviving child of his parents. They had twelve children: and to him appertained the peculiar circumstance of being the first and the last of them all; affording thus a striking instance of the uncertain tenure of life. When he left New York, he had a brother living, and three sisters. They were in health and vigour, and considerably younger than himself. He was feeble and languishing: but, in course of years, they all died; and he lived to mourn the loss of them, and to embalm their memory.

When speaking of the many deprivations which he had sustained, of kind friends and relatives, a circumstance which, in his lengthened life, was inevitable, he often said, in the words of the poet:

> "Our little lights go out by one and one."

But after all his bereavements, he still possessed, as he observed, the uncommon privilege and providential favour of having his beloved wife preserved to him. The continuance of this blessing to the end of his days was inestimable. No one, however kindly disposed, could have supplied to him the place of a most affectionate wife; a constant companion and faithful attendant; a beloved friend, with whom, from his youth, he took sweet counsel on all the concerns of his life. He often said, he had abundant cause to value her very highly, and to consider her as the greatest temporal blessing of his life; and she was indeed fully entitled to his love and esteem.

Mrs. Murray is not a showy nor a literary woman: but she possesses a solid understanding, great firmness of mind, and a particularly kind disposition. To the poor and afflicted, she is, in a high degree, liberal and compassionate. By her skill and prudence in the management of her household affairs, she relieved her husband from all care or anxiety on those subjects. She was most tenderly attached, and even devoted, to him; always preferring his gratification to her own. Her aged and beloved father, and a large circle of relatives and friends, she freely left to accompany her husband into England. For many years after she came into this country, she still called New York her home; but she never requested, or wished, him to return. She encouraged and assisted him, as far as she was able, in every good word and work; and often expressed her solicitous desire, that both she, and her "precious husband," as she frequently called him, "might so pass through this life, as not to fail of future and everlasting bliss;" adding:

"If we are but prepared for that happy state, we need not fear how soon we depart hence." During the latter years of her husband's life, she scarcely ever quitted the house; and very rarely the two rooms occupied by him. She said, she was most comfortable with him; and that if he were taken ill suddenly, as was sometimes the case, she could never forgive herself, if she were absent.

As Mrs. Murray is still living, it may seem indelicate to speak of her in terms thus commendatory. But she is so intertwined with the memory of her husband, that I could not write any account of him without mentioning her; and I could not mention her, except to praise her.

On every anniversary of their marriage, the twenty-second of June, which was also the birthday of his wife, he never failed to congratulate her, on the return of that auspicious day. On some of these occasions, occurring in a late period of their union, he offered his congratulation not only verbally, but also in writing: thus giving additional force, as well as permanence, to the expression of his sentiments. In these written testimonials, which she justly esteems amongst the most valuable of her possessions, he assures her that during the whole period of their union, she has been, by far, his greatest earthly treasure; that, in health and sickness, in prosperous and adverse situations, in all the varied events of

their lives, he has ever found her the same uniform, kind, and faithful friend, the sweetener and improver of every allotment: and he offers her his most grateful acknowledgments for her cordial attachment, and affectionate services; for her kind assiduity, and tender solicitude, to promote his comfort and happiness in every respect.

From these beautiful little effusions of devotional, as well as conjugal feeling, I have pleasure in presenting to the reader, a few extracts; which evince not only Mr. Murray's tender regard for his wife, in the decline of life, but also his increasing piety, his deep humility, and the ground of his hope of finding mercy and acceptance with God.

1809. "This, my beloved Hannah, is the forty-second anniversary of that happy period, when we were joined together in the tender and sacred bonds of wedlock. To me this event has ever proved most auspicious; and I am persuaded that my choice could not have been happier. I have never seen a single moment, that I could have wished my choice had been different.—But a few more, at the most, can be the returns of this happy day. Perhaps not another may be given to us. If that should be the case, let the surviver rather be thankful that so much has been bestowed, than murmur because no more was allowed. It is an inexpressible comfort, that our latter years have been the sweetest to us, though every part of our connexion has been pleasant.

When the time comes, whether sooner or later, that we must part, may the surviver be blessed with the hope and faith, that a little time will reunite us in the blessed abodes: where we shall have, with purified affections and enlarged minds, to sing the praises of our God and Saviour, through the endless ages of eternity."

1812. "This day, my beloved Hannah, it is forty-five years since we were joined together in the pleasant bonds of marriage. I feel grateful to my heavenly Father, for the blessing of so kind, and faithful, and so very suitable a partner.—Our connexion has continued for a much longer period, than is common; and this is an additional source of thankfulness to the bountiful Author of all good. But the longer we have been preserved to each other, the shorter must be the time that remains. May it be studiously improved to the glory of God, and our own final happiness!

It is an inexpressible satisfaction to reflect, that our latter days have been our best days; and that a desire for each other's welfare, has increased as we advanced in life. May our prayers and labours for each other's future felicity, grow more and more ardent, during the remainder of our short time; and may the surviver rather be thankful for the mercies that are past, than dwell mournfully on those which are taken away! A little time after the separation, will, I humbly hope, reunite our spirits in a better world; where we shall glorify, praise, and serve our heavenly Father, Redeemer, and Sanctifier, for endless ages, with enlarged understandings and purified affections, as the greatest happiness, and highest perfection, of which our nature is capable."

1817. "This day, my beloved Hannah, we have been united in the sacred bonds of wedlock, for fifty years, half a century! How very few have lived together so many years, in this happy connexion!—Many are the dangers we have escaped, and the preservations we have experienced, during this length of time, which have been seen and observed by us: but innumerable, perhaps, have been the deliverances and protections, that were unseen and unknown, which a gracious and merciful Providence has extended towards us! For these, and all his mercies and blessings with which we have been favoured, we are bound to praise and glorify Him, to adore, love, and serve Him, most gratefully, during the short remaining period of our lives here; and in his holy and happy kingdom hereafter, if we should be blessed, as I humbly hope we shall, to be partakers of that heavenly inheritance.

May we, my dear Hannah, be very diligent to improve the remaining portion of time, whether it be longer or shorter: so that we may, at last, when the hour of parting comes, have a well founded hope that the season of separation will be short; and take leave of each other, as companions who have been dearly united, and who, through Infinite love and mercy, will be joined again in the mansions of eternal peace; where we shall for ever rejoice together, in praising, adoring, and serving our God and Redeemer, with the highest gratitude and love, of which our enlarged minds shall then be made capable.

In the course of the long period of our union, we have had our trials and afflictions.—But we have been favoured too, with many great and distinguished blessings. Even the afflictions, and what appeared to be adverse occurrences, were designed for our final wellbeing. I hope the gracious intention of these dispensations will be fully answered by our being safely landed, through the atonement and intercession of our blessed Redeemer, on those happy shores, where no clouds nor storms are ever known; and where, after millions of ages of happiness shall have passed away, we shall only seem to have begun our felicity, a felicity that will last for ever.

We know not, my dear Hannah, which of us shall be first removed from this earthly scene;

which of us shall have to lament the loss of a partner so long known and beloved. But whichever of us may be the surviver, let not that surviver mourn as one without hope, but endeavour to perform the remaining duties required; to be humbly resigned to the will of Heaven; and to wait, with patience and hope, for a blessed and happy reunion."

1821. "This day, my beloved Hannah, is the fifty-fourth anniversary of our marriage.— At this late period of our lives, we cannot, in the course of nature, look for a much longer continuance together. Our remaining time here must now be short. Perhaps we may not be permitted to see another anniversary of our union. If this should be the case, or whenever we may be removed from this transient scene, may the God of love and mercy be graciously pleased, through the blessed Redeemer, to give us an inheritance in his holy and happy kingdom; there to be reunited in our spirits, and joyfully employed in thanksgiving and praises, and the most devout and zealous services, to our heavenly Father and Redeemer, for endless ages!

Whichever of us may be the surviver, I hope that Divine Goodness and Mercy will be near, to support that surviver under so deeply trying an event, and to produce a humble, reverent submission to the will of Heaven.—May we both, my dear Hannah, now when the curtains of the night are soon, or before long, to be drawn around us, be more and more diligent to make our calling and election sure; to be prepared for striking our tents, and removing to a better world; where, sinful and unworthy as I am, I hope, through the Infinite mercy of God in Jesus Christ, to be admitted; and where, if admitted, we shall be finally delivered from all sickness and sorrow, from all sin, temptation, and imperfection."

As a further proof of Mr. Murray's piety and humility, I present to the reader the following memorandums; all of which, except the two first, were found in his desk after his decease. They are mere fragments; written on detached slips of paper, some of them only with a pencil: but fragments of such a mind as his, should be gathered up, when it can be done with delicacy and propriety, and without violating any known or expressed wish of the writer. They, as well as the preceding extracts from the little addresses to his wife, are so accordant with the tenour of his Memoirs, that I cannot doubt but that, if he were living, he would give leave for their insertion. Indeed, I think it is not improbable that some of the memorandums were designed as hints or materials for a continuation of the Memoirs;

the original notices with which he furnished me, being written in a similar manner.

"It may be truly asserted, that a tenth part of the solicitude which we have, to secure a precarious happiness, for a few years upon earth, would secure a perfect felicity, for endless ages, in heaven.—How greatly will this consideration increase our anguish at last, if we should neglect in time, to procure, at so easy a sacrifice, the blessedness of a future state!—The summer of 1811."

"Be watchful. Be humble. Be grateful." *

"It is a comfort to me to feel that the longer I live, the greater is my regard for my friends and acquaintance, and my desire that we may all meet in a better world; where we shall, if we attain it, be for ever grateful, beyond expression, to our Divine Benefactor."

"But a little time remains for me, (and how little that may be I know not,) to prepare to meet the God of my life, and to give in to Him an account of my actions."

"I am this day seventy-two years of age. How many preservations and mercies have I ex-

* These words were addressed to his wife: but they were also the daily rule of his own life; and they form a striking summary of Christian duty.

perienced in this long course of time! How poorly I have improved the goodness and forbearance of God to me! What has been the design of this long continuance of life, and of the blessings with which my cup has run over? Plainly, that I might improve these mercies, by gratitude, love, and obedience, to my great Benefactor; and be prepared to enter into his holy and happy kingdom, there to glorify and serve him for ever. May this be my joyful experience, through the mercy of God, in Jesus Christ, and for his sake! I know, by long and repeated proofs in myself, and by the testimony of the Holy Scriptures, that of myself I can do nothing to effect my salvation: my powers are all inadequate to this great end. It is by the Grace of God alone, that the work can be effected. May I ever look to that, and pray for it, and finally experience it to work in me a most comfortable and steadfast hope, that I shall be made one of those holy and happy beings, who shall glorify, adore, praise, and serve Him, for evermore, with the highest degree of love and gratitude, that their enlarged spirits shall then be made capable of exerting."

"Preserve me from all vain self complacencies; from seeking the applauses of men; and from all solicitude about what they may think or say of me. May I be made truly humble, and of a meek and quiet spirit! If I have done any good to my fellow-creatures, or, in any degree, promoted the will of my heavenly Father, may I unfeignedly give him all the glory; attributing nothing to myself, and taking comfort only from the reflection, that an employment in his service, affords an evidence that his mercy is towards me, that I am not forsaken by Him, and that he is training me for an inhabitant of his blessed kingdom, there to glorify and serve my God and Redeemer for ever."

From the conclusion of Mr. Murray's Memoirs, till his decease, his life proceeded in a pretty uniform tenour; little diversified by incident, or by any change of circumstance, except the vicissitude from sickness to a state of comparative health. The power of employing his time to good and useful purposes, was, through a peculiarly benign providence, continued to the latest period of his life. Religious reading and meditation, which, as he advanced in years, became increasingly acceptable to him; the arrangement of his secular affairs both with respect to his continuance in, or removal from, this sphere of action; attention to his literary works; social intercourse; acts of beneficence and charity; were employments which rendered the long evening of his days useful and pleasant.

In the full enjoyment of life, and in the discharge of all its varied and important duties, he attained his eighty-first year: which, considering his long confinement, and his general debility, was a remarkable circumstance; a kind of jubilee in his existence. On his birthday, he appeared so well, and cheerful, and so bright in his mental faculties, that the prospect of losing him seemed as remote as on any similar occasion, during many preceding years. "I am favoured," he piously observed, "with a comfortable state of health, for my time of life; a state for which I ought, and I desire, to be humbly and deeply thankful to the gracious Giver of all good."—But the year which he had so auspiciously begun, he was not allowed to complete. A happier birthday than any which we had anticipated, I doubt not, awaited him.

Persons who were strangers to him, might suppose from his age and long confinement, that, at this period, he was fairly worn out, both in body and mind. But this was by no means the case. His health, towards the close of life, seemed rather to improve. In the autumn and winter immediately preceding his decease, he appeared unusually free from indisposition. His sight and hearing were good. With spectacles, he could read the finest print. His memory, even for recent events, was remarkably retentive.

He appeared as sensible, well-informed, and cheerful, as at any former period during my acquaintance with him. His vigour of mind was unimpaired: he was, indeed, incapable of long-continued attention to any subject; but this seemed rather the effect of bodily than mental decay. His hair had become entirely white: his countenance bespoke age and feebleness; but still retained an expression of mingled intelligence and sweetness.

In October, 1825, I went from home. Having previously informed him of my intention, he expressed, as he had often done before, an earnest desire that I might not be absent at the time of his decease. As his health then seemed better than usual, the expression of this sentiment appeared to me less adapted to the occasion, than his sentiments usually were; and tended, unnecessarily I thought, to cast a gloom and depression over my mind. But the event fully justified him. I had not been returned many weeks, before I visited him on his death-bed, and followed his remains to the grave. That his desire was accomplished; and that I saw him in his last hours, and received from him some token of kind remembrance and parting friendship; are circumstances which afford my mind inexpressible satisfaction.

I was at his house, a very short time before his last illness. When I was about taking leave of him, he said to me: "REMEMBER the following lines." He pronounced the word "Remember," and repeated the lines, with an emphasis, which now assumes something of prophetic energy.

> "Absent or dead, still let a friend be dear:
> A sigh the absent claims; the dead a tear."

On the tenth of January, 1826, Mr. Murray being at dinner, was seized with a slight paralytic affection in his left hand; it was, however, of short duration, and was attended with no visible ill effect. On Monday morning, the thirteenth of February, he had a return of numbness, in the same hand; but it soon yielded to friction, and wholly disappeared. Soon after, he conversed very cheerfully, and even pleasantly. During the day, he was a good deal engaged, and much interested, in having the newspaper read to him, containing the debates on the commercial embarrassments of the country. In the afternoon of that day, the last time of his taking a pen in his hand, I received from him a short note, as kind, as usual, and as well written and composed. That the last words which he ever wrote, were addressed to me, is a melancholy recollection; but it is inexpressibly soothing and consolatory to my mind.

In the evening, he was seized with acute pain in his groin, accompanied with violent sickness. Medical assistance was procured : but the means used to afford relief proved ineffectual. During the night he had an alarming fainting fit, of long continuance. On recovering, he spoke most tenderly to his wife, and urged her to go to bed.

I saw him on the following morning. He then seemed rather better ; but said the pain was not removed. When I was going away, he took leave of me with unusual solemnity, saying, very slowly, and with a most affecting emphasis : "Farewell, my dear friend!" With some difficulty, he extended his hand under the bed clothes, and uncovered it, in order that he might, at parting, shake hands with me.

In the evening, he was conveyed, in his rolling chair, to a bed prepared for him in his sitting room. Some time after, the aperient medicines took effect ; and this circumstance, together with his disposition to sleep, appeared very favourable, and encouraged a hope of his speedy recovery. But he spent a restless night ; and in the morning he was in a state of extreme exhaustion. When his wife went to his bed side, he revived a little ; spoke sweetly to her ; and seeing her soon afterwards, at a little distance in the room, he looked at her very tenderly, and said, "That dear one!" He slumbered most of the morning, except when roused to take refreshment. I visited him about noon. Seeing me at his bed side, and probably being unwilling, though in a state of great weakness, not to notice me, he looked at me very kindly; and repeated my name three times, in a low but affectionate tone of voice; and again stretched forth his hand under the bed clothes, towards me. That hand, which had so kindly welcomed me, when first I entered the room, at the commencement of our acquaintance, was now extended towards me for the last time; not to welcome, but gently to dismiss me. I heard the sound of his voice no more; nor did I ever again behold his living countenance.

In the afternoon, his wife sent me word he was better; and I flattered myself with the hope that he would speedily recover, as I had seen him do on many previous occasions. Great were my surprise and disappointment when I received, on the following morning, the melancholy intelligence that he was much worse. I hastened to his house; but, before I arrived, "his dear spirit," to use his wife's expression, "had taken its flight." Thus terminated an uninterrupted intercourse of many years' standing, with a most excellent man, and a kind friend. The loss to me is irreparable. In this world of sin and error, a true friend is rarely to be met with: "an old friend," as Dr. Johnson observes, "can never be found."

During his short illness, my much esteemed friend expressed his gratitude for the care that was taken of him, and for all the kind attention which he received. He also adverted to the pleasant conversation which he had, on the morning of his seizure; and remarked: "What poor, frail creatures we are; and how little we know what is to happen to us!"

On Wednesday afternoon he seemed refreshed by sleep; noticed what was passing in the room; and took sustenance freely. But the night was again restless. His pulse was quick, and his tongue parched. Though he was evidently suffering from pain, he made very little complaint: when inquired of, he said the pain was still fixed in the same place. A few times, he cried out: "Oh my ——;" but checked himself before the expression was completed.

In the morning, his servant being at his bed side, and tenderly sympathizing with him, told him she should be very glad, if she could afford him any relief from his suffering. He expressed his sense of her kindness; but meekly added: "It is MY portion."

About seven in the morning, a change for the worse evidently took place. Soon after that time, his wife went to his bed side; he noticed her; and spoke to her, in the most tenderly affectionate manner. A deathlike sickness seemed to be coming over him. He cried out: "Oh my groin!—What a pain!" Being asked on which side the pain was, he said: "On the right." His wife warmed a cloth, and put it to the part. He turned on his back, and lay stretched at his length: his arms were extended, close to his body; the thumb of each hand was gently pressed upon the forefinger, seeming to indicate suppressed agony: and in that attitude he continued during the short remainder of his mortal existence. For a few moments, anguish was depicted on his countenance: but it soon gave place to fixed serenity. His eyes were lifted up; no doubt, in fervent supplication to the God of mercy. His lips moved, though no sound of his voice could be heard. He lay without any perceptible motion, until his eyes gently closed of themselves. About half-past eight in the morning, he expired in peace; without a struggle, or even a sigh or a groan.

Thus died, on Thursday morning, the sixteenth of February, 1826, the much loved and much lamented Lindley Murray; in the eighty-first year of his age, and in the full possession of all his mental faculties. His last illness was of short duration, scarcely exceeding two days: but his life, during a long course of years, was a constant preparation for the awful change which has now taken place; so that death could scarcely at any time have come upon him unawares, or found him in a state, unsuited for removal to a world of glory.

The immediate cause of his dissolution cannot be ascertained; nor is it material now. His allotted work was finished: his Lord called him home, to receive his appointed wages. Nor can it be known, whether at any time of his short illness, he was sensible that the close of his earthly existence was at hand. The alternation of pain and extreme exhaustion in which the last days of his life were spent, allowed him little opportunity to say any thing, but what was absolutely necessary respecting the illness of his body. In his final hour, if not before, it is probable, the solemn truth was conveyed to his mind; and his soul was lifted up in fervent prayer, to the Father of spirits, and the God of mercy and consolation. The thoughts, the feelings, of the mind, especially of such a mind as his, when earth and all connected with it, recede from the view, and the eternal world appears, can never be spoken, or fully made known, on this side the grave.

The peculiarly benign providence which had followed him through life, forsook him not in the end. His removal, though a loss to the world at large, and a subject of much regret to his friends, was, no doubt, a dispensation of mercy. He was taken away from the evil to come. He was translated to glory, in the lengthened evening of his day ; but in the midst of usefulness and honour, of comfort and happiness. The powers of his mind were not suffered to waste away, nor to decline into imbecility. The loveliness of his character was not sullied, nor the efficacy of his example impaired, by any infirmity of mind or of body. His old age, to the very latest period of it, was an object, not of commiseration, but of love, esteem, and reverence.

His death was easy, both as regards the body and the soul. The bodily suffering which preceded it, though severe, was not protracted ; nor did it, at any moment, obscure his understanding, or disturb the tranquillity of his mind. His passage through the valley of the shadow of death, was short, and free from terror. He seemed to have no internal conflict. All within appeared calm and tranquil. Devotedness to God, and love to man, were almost the latest expressions of his departing spirit.

His peaceful and happy death formed a natural and beautiful close of his holy and virtuous life. In the extremity of nature, the spirit of the Lord sustained him. The arm of the Lord, though invisible, was underneath him. The Lord was round about him, and made all his bed in his sickness. With filial confidence and love, he rested on the bosom of his heavenly Parent. He died in the Lord; he fell asleep in the Lord Jesus. And he verified the Scripture declaration: "Behold the upright man; and mark the perfect man: for the end of that man is peace." No doubt, the Lord Jesus, in whom he had trusted, and whom he had served, from his youth, received his spirit. And he has now, I trust, begun that celestial song, and entered upon that elevated sphere of action, of which, while on earth, he had joyful and devout anticipation.

> "The chamber where the good man meets his fate,
> Is privileg'd above the common walk
> Of virtuous life, quite on the verge of heav'n.
> His God supports him in his final hour;
> His final hour brings glory to his God." YOUNG.

Mr. Murray, in one of his illnesses, expressed an earnest hope that, at the close of life, whenever it might take place, he should be mercifully supported: so that he might not disgrace religion by any unbecoming words or behaviour; but might even, if enabled by divine grace, glorify God in his dying hours, and edify his fellow-creatures. His wish was, in a good degree, accomplished. He glorified God, I doubt not, by the secret aspirations of his heart; as I am sure he did by his meek, unrepining endurance of pain and weakness, and his kind, considerate attention to all around him. On the minds of the survivers, his affectionate regard for others in the midst of his own sufferings, his quiet resignation, his patient sickness, and his tranquil death, are calculated to produce deep and salutary impressions.

His death, in some of its circumstances, was awfully affecting: it was, in a manner, sudden; and it was, to his friends at least, wholly unexpected. In this respect, also, it is instructive; and, as he wished, edifying to the survivers. It warns them of the uncertainty of life: it admonishes them to prepare, and to live prepared, to meet their Creator and their Judge; and it urges them, by this most cogent reason, not to delay the preparation, seeing they know neither the day, nor the hour, when they will be summoned to the awful tribunal.

> "Thus runs Death's dread commission; 'Strike, but so
> As most alarms the living by the dead.'
> Is death uncertain? therefore thou be fix'd;
> Fix'd as a sentinel, all eye, all ear,
> All expectation of the coming foe.
> Rouse, stand in arms, nor lean against thy spear,
> Lest slumber steal one moment o'er thy soul,
> And fate surprise thee nodding. Watch, be strong:
> Thus give each day the merit, and renown,
> Of dying well; tho' doom'd but once to die.
> Nor let life's period hidden (as from most)
> Hide too from thee the precious use of life." YOUNG.

Though the final summons to the eternal world, vouchsafed to Mr. Murray, was but short, he was, through Infinite mercy, ready to depart. All his concerns, respecting both worlds, were settled and arranged. He was at peace with all men. And he had, I doubt not, a comfortable assurance, as in all former illnesses that, through the merits of the Redeemer, his sins were pardoned, and his transgressions blotted out. If this had not been the case, how dreadful would his condition have been! From the commencement of his short illness till its close, he was incapable of paying attention to any worldly affairs; far less to the great work of salvation. The thought of unsettled business, or of unrepented sins, would, no doubt, in his weak state, have overpowered his reason, or plunged him into the agonies of despair. In this point of view also, his death is edifying; not only to his surviving friends, but to all who may read or hear the account. It is calculated to awaken in their minds, an earnest desire that, through faith in Christ, and through divine grace, they may be enabled to live the life of the righteous; and that when their final summons is sent forth, they may be found, like the excellent Lindley Murray, having finished their allotted work, being at peace with all men, and having a humble trust that the Shepherd of Israel, will, with his rod and staff, conduct them safely, through the valley of the shadow of death, into the land of promise.

Mr. Murray's will, signed Feb. 1, 1821, was written and composed by himself. It affords a striking proof of the vigour of his mind in advanced age, his accuracy in transacting business, and his solicitous desire to do as much and as extensive good, both living and dying, as his circumstances would allow. To make a suitable provision for his wife, and to afford her every comfortable accommodation, seems to be the primary object of his testamentary attention. He mentions in his will a large number of relatives and friends; to each of whom he bequeaths a legacy, either in money, or books, or both: the books are partly to be taken from his own library, and partly to be purchased; and he has, with particular pains, selected and apportioned them in such a manner, as he thought would be most acceptable and useful. To myself he bequeaths, besides some books, all his papers and letters respecting his literary concerns. Several poor persons whom he occasionally employed, or assisted by his alms, are also mentioned in his will; to each of whom he bequeaths the sum of two guineas. He leaves the following charitable bequests, payable after the death of his wife: to the British and Foreign Bible Society, two hundred pounds; to the African Institution, the same sum ; and to each of the following institutions, or societies, at York, twenty-five pounds; the County Hospital, the Dispensary, the Blue Coat School for Boys, the Gray Coat School for Girls, the Charitable Society, the Benevolent Society, and the Lunatic Asylum. After the decease of his wife, and the payment of all his bequests, the residue of his property is to be transferred to New York, and vested in trustees there, so as to form a permanent fund; the yearly income or produce of which is to be appropriated in the following manner: "in liberating black people who may be held in slavery, assisting them when freed, and giving their descendants, or the descendants of other black persons, suitable education; in promoting the civilization and instruction of the Indians of North America; in the purchase and distribution of books tending to promote piety and virtue, and the truth of Christianity; and it is his wish that 'The Power of Religion on the Mind, in Retirement, Affliction, and at the Approach of Death,' with the author's latest corrections and improvements, may form a considerable part of those books; and in assisting and relieving the poor of any description, in any manner that may be judged proper, especially those who are sober, industrious, and of good character."

On Wednesday morning, the twenty-second of February, Mr. Murray's remains were interred in the burying ground of the Friends, or Quakers, in the city of York; amidst a large assemblage of persons, many of whom had come from a considerable distance. From the stillness which prevailed, one might have thought only few persons were present. All were silent and serious; many deeply affected.

No relative was present. His aged and bereaved widow, though entirely resigned to the Divine will, was, from affliction, indisposition, and long confinement, unable to attend. All his own relations, and those of his wife, were resident in America. The intelligence of his death could not reach them, till long after his remains were consigned to the silent grave. A large number of his friends, acquaintance, and other persons, followed his corpse to the place of interment; and were truly mourners. Few have departed this life more beloved and lamented: the graves of few have been surrounded by so many persons, who, if they had been allowed to speak, could have told of some favour or benefit, some good advice or kind attention, which they had received from the deceased; or could, in some way or other, either directly or indirectly, have acknowledged him as their friend and benefactor. And thousands who were absent, might, if their voice could have been heard, have joined in the acknowledgment.

His life and death were blessed, and his memory is blessed. He had great talents imparted to him, and high success attended him in the employment of them. By his virtues and his kindness, he will long live in the affectionate and grateful remembrance of his friends and acquaintance. His literary works and his good deeds are a lasting memorial of him. His name, wherever the English language is spoken, (and soon, where will it not be spoken?) will be known and revered. The little tribute to his memory which I now present to the world, will, I hope, contribute to make him valued and remembered, not only as Lindley Murray, the Grammarian, as he is usually designated; but, in a far higher character, as Lindley Murray, the benevolent and pious; the friend of man, and the faithful, dedicated servant of the Lord God Omnipotent.

CHAPTER II.

CHARACTER OF THE AUTHOR.

THE character of the author is depicted in his writings, particularly in his Memoirs. And it is deeply engraven on the memories of many, who were personally acquainted with him; or who have derived benefit from his literary labours. But it was so excellent, and in many respects, so imitable, that, as editor of his Memoirs, I cannot feel excused from attempting a delineation; which I shall intersperse with various illustrative anecdotes. It will thus assume rather an historical form; but, I trust, it will not, on that account, be the less interesting.

Mr. Murray seems to have been raised up by Providence, for peculiar purposes: to do good in the world, and to exhibit a beautiful specimen of a Christian character. His endowments, both moral and intellectual, were of a superior order. Few men have left behind them a higher character for wisdom, piety, and benevolence.

Good sense and sound judgment were the predominating qualities of his mind. He took a large, comprehensive, and accurate view of the objects presented to his mental eye; and he discerned, clearly and readily, which of those objects were to be preferred and pursued. His apprehension was quick; his memory retentive; and his taste delicate and refined. There did not appear in any of the faculties of his mind, either exuberance or deficiency. Their general harmony, as well as strength, constituted the distinguishing excellence of his intellectual character.

To the appellation of a man of genius, he has an undoubted claim; if true genius signifies, according to the definition of a celebrated author, "a mind of large, general powers, accidentally," or rather providentially, "determined to some particular direction."—The strength of his intellect, and the habit of close, vigorous application which he acquired early in life, enabled him, at will, to collect his thoughts, and to fix them wholly, and for a sufficient length of time, on any subject under his consideration. Hence, whatever he did, was well done, and with comparative ease. And hence too, he would have excelled in every pursuit in which he had engaged, or on whatever subject to which he had turned his attention. His grammatical works have obtained so much celebrity, and they exhibit so high a degree of excellence, that it might not unreasonably be supposed, grammar was the principal study of his life; but it did not particularly engage his attention, until a short time previous to the publication of his first work on that subject.

Before he began any literary work, or engaged in any undertaking, he considered what was useful, practicable, and excellent. His imagination did not bewilder him with a diversity of plans and views. A few obvious and judicious means of accomplishing the end proposed, immediately presented themselves to his mind. These he considered with attention; selected from them what he thought best; and then proceeded to action, without any agitating hope of success, or fear of failure. He pursued a straight forward path; not unnecessarily retracing his steps, nor wasting his powers in idle wanderings, or useless cogitations. He formed a grand outline of what he proposed, from which he seldom deviated: then he filled up all the parts successively; overcoming the difficulties as they occurred, and, on no account, suffering them to accumulate. He never undertook any thing to which he was not more than equal; and he seldom relinquished any thing which he had undertaken.

He composed, and wrote, with quickness and accuracy. His Grammar, as it appeared in the first edition, was completed in rather less than a year. It was begun in the spring of 1794, and it was published in the spring of 1795; though he had an intervening illness, which, for several

weeks, stopped the progress of the work. Afterwards, indeed, he bestowed much attention, and a considerable portion of time, in improving and enlarging the work for a second, and many subsequent editions. The Exercises and Key were also composed in about a year: and none of his succeeding publications engrossed, in the first instance, a larger portion of time.

His handwriting was uncommonly and uniformly neat. "Indeed," as was once justly observed of him, "he was neat and accurate in every thing he did." I present my readers with a fac simile of a few lines written by him on his last birthday, June 7, 1825.—In 1823, he revised and wrote a fair copy of his Memoirs. This manuscript, from which they are printed, is, as well as his will, a beautiful specimen of neat and correct handwriting, at a very advanced period of life. It is throughout perfectly legible: it has no blots, and but few erasures or interlineations.

Mr. Murray's sentiments were elevated and refined; his ideas and opinions just and well founded; and always expressed in delicate and appropriate language. They often attracted attention by their novelty: accompanied with a conviction of their propriety, in the minds of those to whom they were communicated; together with some degree of surprise that they had not previously occurred, or at least not with so strong an evidence of their justness. Both in writing and speaking, his manner of expression was simple and pleasing, but correct and accurate, clear and concise: no one could be at a loss to understand his meaning, or to apprehend its force. He had a happy choice of words, and a clear arrangement of his thoughts; avoiding all useless repetition, or awkward, unnecessary explanation, and all contradiction or inconsistency. The current of his expressions and thoughts was easy and natural, smooth and regular.

The powers of his mind were improved and enlarged, not only by study, reading, and reflection, but also by observation, and by extensive intercourse with mankind. His early introduction to business, and the diversity of employment in which he was subsequently engaged, gave him an insight into human affairs; and contributed, no doubt, very essentially, to improve and exercise his judgment, and to store his memory with various and useful information. His observations on what he saw in the world, and his reflections on what passed in his own mind, gave him an accurate knowledge of human nature.

In his Memoirs, he seems to undervalue his acquirements, particularly his classical and literary attainments. He had a considerable acquaintance with the Latin and French languages, and some knowledge of Greek. He was an excellent arithmetician and accountant. With general literature, including history and geography, he was well acquainted. He used to say, though not designing to disparage what is called learning, that if he had been intimately acquainted with ancient languages, he might, perhaps, by introducing much curious and recondite matter, into his grammatical and other works, have rendered them less useful and acceptable. The general scholar, and the man of business, do not require to know the remote etymologies of words, but their present meaning, and their right application and arrangement. Mr. Murray seemed to have acquired all the general knowledge which is practically useful. But his knowledge, though general, was not superficial. What he knew, he knew well. One of his early instructers said of him: "Il veut tout approfondir." And this character he retained to the end of life, with respect to every object which he deemed worthy of his serious attention. On whatever subject of general importance or interest, that occurred in conversation, or in the business of life, he either possessed all the requisite information; or he could readily obtain it, by a reference to some written authority, or by judicious questions and observations addressed to those with whom he was conversing. Even in his retirement at Holdgate, he was much consulted on matters of law and literature, morals and religion ; the forming and conducting of public and private institutions ; and, indeed, on all subjects of importance in themselves, or in the view of those who consulted him. The opinion which he gave, was, on most occasions, just ; and satisfactory to those by whom it was requested.

His disposition was uncommonly active. When he became incapable of bodily exertion, he turned, with alacrity, to pursuits purely intellectual. His friends sometimes expressed their apprehension that his close application to literary employments, might, in his weak state of health, prove injurious to him ; he would pleasantly say : "It is better to wear away, than to rust away."

He had an even flow of spirits, and great cheerfulness of temper. He seems to have been naturally mild, gentle, and compassionate, yet firm, steadfast, and resolute. To the latest period of his life, he possessed lively sensibility, warmth of feeling, and tenderness of affection.

He exercised great and habitual self control. All his feelings and emotions were, as far as human imperfection will allow, subjugated by reason and religion. He was quick in discerning, and solicitous to check, the risings of evil passions, and to refrain, as far as possible, from acting under their influence. He seldom suffered any circumstance, or event, to ruffle his temper, or disturb his rest. And it may almost be remarked of him, as of an eminent statesman, that " he could cast off his cares with his clothes."

His joys and griefs, his hopes and fears, his purposes and desires, on all occasions on which I ever witnessed them, were tempered, partly by native mildness, and partly by religious considerations. The delicacy of taste and feeling, which he cultivated, seemed to have a considerable effect in inducing a certain nicety and caution, and the avoidance of error and excess, both moral and intellectual. He was free from that vain inflation of mind, and self sufficiency, which too often accompany and disgrace talents; and he was equally removed from despondence, or a groundless distrust of the abilities which he possessed. Of his own character, he formed a just, though humble estimate; preserving a due medium between pride on the one hand, and degradation on the other.

He entertained a high sense of moral obligation. His probity was unimpeachable. He neither allowed nor tolerated in himself, a departure, in any degree, or on any occasion, from strict integrity. In all his transactions, particularly of a pecuniary nature, he was scrupulously exact: careful to take no unfair advantage, to evade no rightful claim, and to omit or delay no just payment, whether with respect to government or any public body, or to individuals. Both in narration and assertion, he considered it an indispensable duty to adhere inviolably to truth ; even on small matters, and on points that are too generally deemed of little moment. He was careful to make no promise or engagement which he could not fulfil ; nor any profession, which he could not justify by his actions, or by the genuine feelings of his heart.

His tender and humble spirit was the proper soil in which religion could take deep root, and flourish.—Often did the tear of sensibility glisten in his eyes, when he heard, or read, affecting passages from the Scriptures, and other writings ; particularly those which, in pointing out the excellent uses of affliction, applied very forcibly to his own state, and to the feelings of his own mind.

From childhood to the latest period of his life, he was, in a high degree, susceptible of religious impressions.—The sun of righteousness appeared in the early morning of his days ; shone, as it advanced, with increasing splendour, and set in brightness : and it has now, I trust, arisen in that morning without clouds, which ushers in a day of never-ending, effulgent glory.

In early life, Mr. Murray was remarkably lively. He engaged in many pursuits and amusements, which his improved reason, and sense of religious duty, afterwards condemned. But he was never a slave to amusement; never allowed himself in any that is absolutely sinful; and never became corrupt in principle, or negligent of the duties of life. His buoyant spirits, his ardent affections, and his superior intellect, rendered his society much courted, and gave a high zest to social enjoyment. His profession of the law, and his widely extended family connexions, naturally led him into company, and not unfrequently into parties of pleasure. He entered into the gaieties of the passing scene, with more spirit and animation than most others did, because he brought to them a purer mind, and he considered them only as relaxations from study or business. But so correct was his conduct, that his companions, who were less restrained than himself, used not unfrequently to say: "Mr. Murray, you are a spy upon us!" and they commented on his moderation and self control, sometimes sarcastically, sometimes with merited commendation. On some occasions, he may have exceeded the bounds of the strictest temperance and self command: yet he was never intoxicated; and but two or three times in a condition, in any degree, approaching to it.

Doubtless, it is to his circumspection under the trials of youth, that he owed much of the future comfort, happiness, and respectability of his life. Few, I believe, have mixed so much in the gay and busy scenes of the world, and retained a more pure, benevolent, and pious spirit, and a more unblemished character. The philosopher who has just notions of the excellence of virtue, will applaud his wisdom, his calm self possession, and his almost complete triumph over the seductions of pleasure. The Christian will observe in them, as in every appearance of nature, every event in human life, the guiding and protecting hand of a most wise and merciful Providence.

Mr. Murray often acknowledged preservation from the snares of youth, as one of the greatest blessings of his life. "I stood," said he, "on the brink of a precipice; and, through Infinite mercy, I was preserved from falling into it." On one occasion, having taken an affecting review of his early life, he added, with deep humility: "I have abundant cause of thankfulness to God, that he has preserved me through those dangerous scenes of folly; and has mercifully enabled me, in some degree, to live to his praise; and to cherish a hope, that I shall answer the great end of my existence, by glorifying and serving him for ever."

Mr. Murray regularly attended public worship, as long as his health would permit; and often even when his weakness, and extreme susceptibility of cold, rendered his attendance rather hazardous. His behaviour, on such occasions, was suited to the solemnity of them; and his countenance bespoke at once the calm, collected, and devout frame of his mind.

He had a great and increasing regard for the sabbath. He was highly sensible of the propriety, and even necessity, of a due observance of it: considering it as a day peculiarly set apart for social worship, and private meditation; a day of rest from worldly business; of suspension, as far as possible, from worldly care; and of preparation, by religious exercises and services, for that happy world, where the redeemed of the Lord celebrate a perpetual sabbath.—One small instance of his reverence for the sabbath may not improperly be adduced. He took much pleasure in reading a daily newspaper: but that he might not, on any occasion of peculiar interest, be induced to look into it, on the sabbath day, he did not, on that day, receive it into his house; but read, or heard read, two papers on the following day. In one of his manuscripts, he observes: "The public worship of the Almighty is a special duty of all men; resulting from the relation in which we all stand to God, as our Creator, Preserver, and Benefactor. Common benefits demand common and united thanksgivings and praises.—That this great duty ought to be frequently performed, is evident, from the nature of it, and the end which it has in view. If a day of religious rest and social worship, did not often occur, there would be danger, that the sense of gratitude to God, and of entire dependance upon him, would languish, if not expire, in the minds of men.—That the observance of a weekly sabbath is entitled to distinguished regard, and is supported by Divine authority, appears from its being a part of the ten commandments; and written, as with the hand of God, on tables of stone, among moral precepts of the highest importance. If an institution of this kind had not been intimately connected with the religious welfare of men, it would not have been classed, in such a manner, with duties of the most interesting nature."

Mr. Murray had a full conviction of the Divine truth and efficacy of Christianity. This conviction commenced with the early dawn of reason; and continued, through life, with unshaken and even increasing force. It was so satisfactory to himself, that he was solicitous to impress it on others. But he never made a wordy profession; seeming to bear in mind the Scriptural admonition: "God is in heaven, and thou upon earth; therefore, let thy words be few." He never obtruded his sentiments; nor lessened their force by pressing them on unsuitable occasions: at the same time, he did not shrink from any opportunity of paying homage to Divine truth, or of supporting it to the utmost of his power. He never spoke on religious subjects, for form sake, or as a matter of course; but always with calmness, seriousness, and reverence. Whatever he said, seemed to flow from the feeling of his heart, and the conviction of his understanding.

But religion with him was not confined to a barren assent of the mind, or to occasional feeling. He experienced, and, with pious simplicity, evinced, its renewing, purifying, and sanctifying influence. It formed his character; it regulated his conduct; it cherished and directed his talents; it enlarged his views and affections; it elevated his thoughts, his hopes, and desires, from earth to heaven. He lived in a confirmed belief of the general and immediate agency of Providence; in a spirit of prayer; and in constant, daily trust in God, and dependance on his care and goodness.

He regarded the Holy Scriptures with profound veneration and love; as the rule of life and faith, and the record of Divine goodness to fallen, sinful man. He read them; he meditated on them; he recommended them to others;

he esteemed it a favour to be enabled, in any degree, to promote the knowledge and circulation of them.—A Bible which he sent to a young friend, was accompanied with the following, among many other observations: "How great a privilege it is, to be blessed with so clear and important communications of the Divine will! which at once enlighten and enlarge the understanding, warm and animate the heart, and continually present to the religious mind, a defence, support, and comfort, under all the trials and vicissitudes of life. It is the secret influence of the divine Spirit alone, which can effectually bless and sanctify the perusal of these invaluable books; and make them a feast more truly rational and delightful, than can be afforded by the most finished human compositions, that ever were exhibited." On recommending the Bible Society to an affluent friend; he said: "Should we not count it a privilege that we can, in any degree, promote the dear Redeemer's kingdom?"

Among men, Mr. Murray knew his comparative worth; he felt and maintained his dignity: but before the Omnipotent he was prostrate in spirit, and deeply humbled; all his honours were laid low; all his good deeds forgotten; he implored mercy, pardon, and help; he pleaded only the merits of the Redeemer. Whilst the world admired him, whilst his most intimate friends and acquaintance revered him, and could scarcely find any fault in him; it appears plainly, from many passages in his Memoirs, from the extracts which I have given, in the preceding chapter, from his manuscripts, and from his verbal declarations on many occasions, that he deeply mourned his transgressions; he felt and lamented his weakness, his infirmity, and his sinfulness; he acknowledged that he had no hope of deliverance from sin, and of eternal happiness, but through the atonement and intercession of the ever blessed Redeemer.

Though highly gifted, and eminently successful in the exercise of his talents, he never arrogated any merit to himself; but, in great humility, attributed all the means with which he had been blessed of doing good in the world, to that gracious Power from whom they had been derived. The following sentiment, though expressed by him on a particular occasion, was, I believe, habitual, whenever he contemplated any good, which he had been the instrument in the hands of Providence of accomplishing: "I feel humbled in spirit; and I adore the condescension of that Great Being, who deigns to employ so feeble and undeserving a creature in the advancement of his work."

The chastened feeling with which he contemplated the great success of his literary productions, and the reputation which they procured for him, is strikingly displayed in the meditation, or prayer, inserted in the preceding chapter.—He was, certainly, much gratified at the distinguished approbation which his works received, and at their uncommon sale. But the pleasure which he felt, was, I believe, unconnected with the gratification of pride or vanity. It seemed only to animate him to fresh exertions; and to excite renewed gratitude to the Giver of all good, and the Disposer of all events. "I hope," said he, "that the praises, both public and private, which I have received, have not, in any degree, puffed me up with pride; or made me contemptuous in my treatment, or opinion, of others, more worthy, but less distinguished, than myself."

On another occasion, having mentioned the extensive sale and high reputation of his works, he added: "I hope that this flattering success has no improper effect upon me. I am sure that my manifold imperfections are sufficient to check elation of mind, and make me humble. I do, indeed, feel grateful to the Author of all good, that, under my long-continued bodily infirmities, I am not yet a useless being in the world."

During the course of a severe though short illness, which brought the prospect of death very near to him, he said to me: "It is a pleasing, though affecting consideration, that when I am mouldering in the dust, thousands will probably be perusing my books; and, I hope, deriving from them moral and religious instruction, and treasuring up in their minds sentiments that will influence their future conduct." On the same occasion, he said: "I own I have been pleased, but, I trust, not improperly, with the general approbation and acceptance which my literary labours have received. But if I know my own heart, my satisfaction arises from the belief that my works are useful; and that the wide circulation of them will tend to the promotion of virtue and piety. Whatever literary reputation I may possess, is certainly derived from my grammatical works: but the chief, if not the only, satisfaction, which I now feel, or which I ever have felt in the hour of serious reflection, from the publication of them, arises from the consideration, that the elements of our language may now be acquired, not only without injury to morals, but they are made the means of infusing into the young mind, sentiments of the best and noblest kind. Had I only taught how to put words together, I could not, at this awful hour, have reflected on my literary labours with that satisfaction which I now feel.—I do not mention these things, or consider them, as merits, in the eyes of my great Creator and Judge. If they were weighed in the balance with my manifold transgressions, they would be found light indeed."

Mr. Murray's resignation, under suffering and privation, and under all the trials of life, was remarkable. He seemed to have no repining or vexatious thoughts that he deserved better of the Supreme Ruler than he received; nor was he grieved when he saw others possessed of advantages, which were withheld from him. His amiable disposition, as well as his sense of religious duty, induced him, at all times, to make the best of his condition, and to look at the bright side of surrounding objects. Both in his letters and in his conversation, he often expressed himself to the following purport: "I am persuaded that Infinite Goodness knows what is best for me; and has assigned me my proper allotment. In his merciful appointment I acquiesce.—To his will I desire humbly and cheerfully to resign myself and all my concerns.—It is a blessing that I am preserved from repining at my condition. I have, indeed, no cause for murmuring; but much for deep humiliation and unceasing thankfulness." All the ills that befell him, he received, with gentleness and submission, as trials or chastisements; and often mentioned them as blessings in disguise.

He bore all his afflictions with the most exemplary patience; particularly many very severe illnesses, and, during a long course of years, almost continued weakness and languor. But even in this respect he fell short of apprehended duty; and he used not unfrequently to lament that he could not attain greater devotedness to the Divine will, and bear bodily pain and suffering with more composure of mind. In a very violent illness which he had in America, (a constipation of the bowels,) feeling excruciating pain, he held forth his hand, and gently snapped his fingers, in a manner, and with an expression of countenance, which indicated, that his sufferings were almost beyond his power of endurance; but he uttered not a word.—Debility and confinement must have been, in the commencement at least, a sore trial and grievous affliction, to a person distinguished as Mr. Murray had been by health, strength, and agility. But never, I believe, did a murmur or complaint, on this or any other account, issue from his lips, or arise in his heart.

I do not think that any of his afflictions, even when they pressed hard upon him, diminished, in the slightest degree, his love and reverence for the Supreme Being. Gratitude seemed to be the predominant and warmest affection which he felt for the Almighty; praise and thanksgiving his favourite theme. He was grateful for every thing: for his afflictions, because they brought him nearer to God and heaven; and for his blessings, because they were an earnest of Divine favour and goodness. He often expressed a fervent desire that all his trials and afflictions might be sanctified to him; and all his blessings carefully numbered, and gratefully acknowledged. But though so resigned to whatever befell him of an afflictive nature, and so patient and contented under it, few persons enjoyed the blessings of life more feelingly than he did; few were more grateful to the Supreme Dispenser of good. All his enjoyments were heightened by reflection, and by a tender sense of obligation to his heavenly Benefactor.

Both in sickness and in health, he often spoke of his own death, in terms at once calm, serious, and affecting; but never, in the slightest degree, indicating any unmanly or unchristian fear. His affectionate disposition, his lively sensibility, and the many blessings which he enjoyed, rendered life very pleasant to him; he valued it highly; and he took all judicious means to preserve and prolong it: but during all the years in which I was acquainted with him, and I believe, long before, he seemed ready, at any moment, to resign it into the hands of the great Bestower, in hopes of a better life, and a more glorious inheritance.

Once, when recovering from an alarming illness, he said: "My life, upon the whole, has been a comfortable one; and marked by many blessings. I have had my afflictions; but these have doubtless been intended for my good. I have felt them to be so; and some of them, I hope, I have properly improved." On the same occasion, he said: "I have had an admonition; a very gentle one. I trust I shall not soon forget it.—I wish to be prepared for death; and to be more and more weaned from life, and all its enjoyments."

He had near and affecting views of a future state of blessedness; and often discoursed on the subject with animation. He believed that the happiness of heaven consists in the enlargement of the faculties of the mind, and the complete purification of the heart; in the adoration of the Supreme Being, with a clear understanding of his wonderful wisdom and goodness; in communion with the spirits of just men made perfect; in administering, in some way or other, to the happiness of God's creatures; and in extending the boundaries of his most righteous, holy, and wise government. He believed, in common with most pious persons, that in a state of blessedness, the soul retains a general consciousness of its previous existence on earth; and also renews virtuous affections and friendships, but only in such a way as is freed from every thing painful, debasing, or inconsistent with perfect bliss and purity.

Being congratulated on one of his birthdays, he replied: "Many returns of this anniversary, I cannot have: but I have a humble trust, that, through the mercy of God in Jesus Christ, I shall be made one of those happy beings, who are employed in his service in the realms of light and joy; and who perform that service with the utmost alacrity; feeling it to be their highest honour and privilege, to do the will, and promote the cause, of their most gracious Lord and Father."

In the last of his little anniversary addresses to his wife, written in his eighty-first year, he says: "For the mercies of preservation, and the continuance of the many blessings we have had together, we have abundant cause to be thankful to our heavenly Protector and Father. May He be pleased to prepare us for his holy and happy kingdom; where we shall then have to rejoice for ever, in rendering continual thanksgivings and praises, and the most devout and zealous services, to our heavenly Father, Redeemer, and Sanctifier, one God, blessed for ever!"

In one of his manuscripts, he observes: "If it would be a circumstance of satisfaction, that the redeemed shall be with the patriarchs whom they never knew; may we not believe that it will also be peculiarly rejoicing to meet those whom they did know and love?

No doubt there will be many new and great sources of joy, to those who are admitted into the realms of bliss: but may we not reasonably believe that *one* of those sources will be the re-union of those who loved one another here, and promoted each other's best interests on earth?—Could they know one another in a happy state, and remember the spiritual strength and comfort, given and received in the days of trial and trouble below, without partaking of a pure and lively joy in the eternal deliverance and happiness of one another?"

Mr. Murray was a member of the society of Quakers, or Friends: by whom he was much respected and esteemed, and justly considered as one of their brightest ornaments. From his earliest years, he was educated in the principles of that society, to which he uniformly adhered. In his conduct and conversation, except in some instances in early life, he conformed to all the peculiarities of the sect; but always with his accustomed delicacy, and regard to the feelings of others. Though attached to his own sect, he had a great respect for truly religious persons of every denomination: he considered them, and often spoke of them, as members of one church, children of one holy and blessed family, and fellow-travellers to a heavenly country. Some of his nearest relations, and many of his friends, were not Quakers; this circumstance probably tended, in no small degree, to preserve him from a spirit of bigotry. But his enlarged views both of divine and human nature, were sufficient, independently of any other consideration, to guard him from the extravagant opinion, which lurks in the minds of some, even pious persons, that to their own sect or party, belong exclusively all virtue and wisdom, all piety and acceptance with God. "Various," Mr. Murray observed, "are the shades and degrees of our understandings and natural dispositions: but if the holy principle is suffered to rule, it will make them all acceptable to Him who framed them, though it may not model them to any standard of uniformity. We are long in learning to judge wisely of one another; and to make charitable allowances for difference of understanding, disposition, education, &c. Mankind are all brethren, the children of one Father: they should, therefore, when we believe them sincere and upright, be received as fellow-partakers of the same privileges."

On another occasion, he observed: "I respect

piety and virtue wherever I meet them. It would be a proof of my own superficiality or depravity, if I valued a truly religious man the less, for the name and profession which he sustains. I trust that I shall ever be influenced by the cheering sentiment, that every man who sincerely loves God and works righteousness, is accepted by him, and is entitled to universal esteem and regard."

In all the varied relations of life, Mr. Murray's conduct was excellent. He was attentive to every dictate of affection, and every requirement of duty. He understood well the nature and extent of all his relative duties; he had reflected much upon them; and he seemed to take pleasure in performing them. He possessed, in an uncommon degree, the respect and affection of all with whom he was intimately connected. Few persons ever left their native land, more beloved and regretted by numerous relations and friends, or took with them more blessings, and good wishes. During the whole time of his residence in this country, though long and far separated from his relatives, he preserved a most affectionate remembrance of them; he rendered them all the varied services and assistance which circumstances would allow; and he kept up with them a regular and frequent correspondence. He said, no time, nor distance, weakened his tender attachment for them.

To his parents, particularly to his mother, he was very affectionate. And he was also highly obedient and respectful ; except perhaps in a few instances in early life, in which the vivacity of his temper, and the peculiarity of his circumstances, may have betrayed him into some violation of filial duty. To his brother and sisters he was uniformly kind and attentive.

As a husband, he was tenderly affectionate, and indulgent. He was the revered guide, and beloved friend, of his wife ; her constant monitor ; her counsellor in difficulty ; her comforter in affliction. She often said : "I believe it is not possible for any woman to have a kinder or more affectionate husband than I have. I hope there are many husbands as good as he is : but I cannot conceive, or allow, that any can be better." They lived together, upwards of fifty-eight years, in uninterrupted harmony. They had no offspring : but neither this circumstance, nor any other, diminished their mutual affection, or their happiness. During the first years of their union, Mr. Murray rather wished for children : but he was perfectly satisfied with the allotment of Providence, in this, as well as in every other respect. He used to say pleasantly that his books were his children ; that, he hoped, they were well settled, and doing good, in the world; and that they had occasioned him less trouble and anxiety than most children give to their parents.

He was a humane and kind master. He did not dispense with the performance of necessary or proper duty; but he exercised authority with moderation, forbearing threatening, and all rude or harsh expressions. He never grudged his servants the well earned reward of their services, or any suitable indulgence; and was always desirous that they should have full time and opportunity, not only to attend public worship, but to all their secular and spiritual concerns. He never required, or looked for, more diligence from them, than could reasonably be expected; and in all their faults and failures, he made due allowance for them, as beings partaking of the same frail nature as himself, but exposed to peculiar temptations and disadvantages. He frequently gave them advice, and moral or religious instruction, adapted to their particular characters and tempers. When they had left his service, he did not forget or forsake them: he continued to bestow upon them such marks of attention, or of pecuniary assistance, as their respective circumstances required. One of his servants, who had lived in his family eight years, being questioned as to her future prospects in life, said: "I never expect to find a better place, nor a better master and mistress." The servant who lived with him at the time of his decease, said: "I believe no person's servants are more comfortably accommodated, in health, or more tenderly cared for, in sickness, than I am."—After Mr. Murray gave up his carriage, which, from his own confinement and that of his wife, had become useless, he kept only one regular, stated servant. His family, for some years previous to his decease, consisted, besides himself and his wife, of one servant, and a female friend, who lived with them as a companion; and who was much employed in reading to them, and in assisting Mrs. Murray in her household concerns. Both these persons, at the time of his decease, had resided in his family nearly twelve years. He has left them, by his will, a handsome acknowledgment of their services, and of his regard. They respected him, during his lifetime, and lamented him, after his death, as a father and a friend.

The praise of conscientious servants and inmates, may justly be considered as the highest panegyric that private virtue can receive. That praise Mr. Murray obtained in a high degree: for, I believe, no servant ever lived with him, and no person ever resided in his house, either as an inmate, or an occasional guest, who did not highly respect him, and speak of him in terms of the warmest commendation.

He was a kind and sincere friend. He highly esteemed his friends; he took pleasure in their company: but so just was the estimate which he formed of human life and character, that he entertained no unreasonable expectations from them. With great delicacy and judgment, he performed towards them the best offices of friendship. He admonished and advised them; he assisted them in their difficulties; he consoled them in their afflictions; and, which is perhaps the severest test of friendship, he bore patiently with their weaknesses and foibles, though perfectly sensible of them, and he usually concealed from others the faults he saw. Few men, none certainly in so retired a situation, ever had so many friends, or was so much beloved by them. He engaged their warmest attachment, and excited in their minds a peculiarity and intenseness of interest. "We felt for him," said one of his friends, after his decease, "as we did for no one else." "In other persons, however estimable," said another of his friends, "we can observe errors, defects, inconsistencies: in him, we could discern nothing but what was amiable, just, and proper."

Enemies, personal enemies, I believe, he had none. Competitors in his literary career, he certainly had: but he practised great forbearance towards them; and always spoke of them with respect and moderation. One of the first of his manuscripts which caught my attention after his decease, contains the following candid observations: "I not only feel myself very much obliged to my friends, for their kind and judicious private remarks on my grammatical works; but I owe something to the public criticisms of several persons who are not very friendly to these publications. Their strictures have enabled me sometimes to correct a real error, and often to remove doubt, and prevent misapprehension."

Mr. Murray was a most pleasing, as well as instructive companion. His voice, though not strong, was clear; and his enunciation remarkably distinct and correct. So great was the versatility of his parts, that he could, with ease, enter into all sorts of conversation of a general and useful nature. His discourse was attractive and interesting even to children and ignorant persons. With wonderful dexterity and condescension, he drew forth from the rich stores of his reading and experience, facts, anecdotes, and observations, tending to recommend some moral precept, or to impress some useful information. When he had young visiters, he not unfrequently introduced some book or paper, which he requested them to read aloud: thus diversifying their entertainment, enlarging their ideas, and suggesting to them new subjects of useful and interesting conversation.

In general discourse, he did not talk much, nor long together, except on business or occasions which rendered it necessary; indeed, he was usually prevented by the weakness of his voice. He seldom said more than the subject required; nor, apparently, more than he intended. He never seemed to talk for the sake of self display, or self gratification. To please or edify those with whom he conversed, or to obtain from them such useful information as they were capable of affording, were his favourite objects.

Subjects of importance were most congenial to his mind. These he frequently introduced; and he seldom failed to represent them in a new and striking point of view, indicating the strength and originality of his mind. He was unassuming in opinion; he never contended eagerly in support of it: but, at the same time, he renounced no important truth, or just principle. The general tenour of his conversation may not unaptly be described in the following lines of the poet:

> "Still turn'd to moral virtue was his speech;
> And gladly would he learn, and meekly teach."

He seemed to hold in his hand the master key of the heart and understanding of those with whom he conversed, or with whom he had to do; and he could, at will, draw forth such tones, grave or gay, soft or strong, as suited the present occasion: but he used this power only for good and legitimate purposes; to allay anger, to sooth discontent, to inspire good resolutions, to prompt judicious decisions. With peculiar aptitude, he discovered, and called forth, the best qualities, the best thoughts and feelings, of those with whom he conversed; these he particularly addressed and cherished: so that in his presence, I have often seen the thoughtless become grave; the profligate, serious; the dull, animate; the timid, free; and the reserved, communicative.

He had a happy art of conveying instruction, reproof, or advice. Instruction he gave with precision, unincumbered with any extraneous matter; reproof he administered with tenderness; advice, with persuasive gentleness. No one, on consulting him, or receiving information from him, could feel humbled, or self abased. He never exulted in the superiority of his knowledge or wisdom. He was slow to contradict, and still slower to blame. He listened patiently; and he did not attempt to answer, or to give an opinion, till he understood the matter. He never exclaimed at the folly, ignorance, or perversity, of those who consulted him, however inwardly convinced of it. He quietly ascertained the extent of their capacity: he observed where their difficulty, or misapprehension lay; and what obstacles pride, passion, or prejudice, placed in the way of truth. By argument clearly and forcibly expressed, by gentle persuasion, or by innocent pleasantry, he seldom failed to win them over to right decision, or proper feeling.

His letters, like his conversation, seemed dictated by a spirit of wisdom and of kindness. On subjects of business, they were explicit and concise; on matters in which self was concerned, delicate and cautious; on occasions of giving advice or admonition, (which sometimes occurred even with regard to strangers,) full of candour and tenderness, yet firm and decisive. Sentiments of piety were so deeply impressed on his own mind, that he could not fail to endeavour, by letter as well as in words, to communicate the impression to others. His letters, even on mere business, frequently contained some sentiment, or expression, calling to the mind of the persons addressed, the concerns of another and a better world. His correspondence was voluminous; and the number of persons to whom he wrote, very great. His separation from his relations, and his literary concerns, independently of other circumstances, naturally gave occasion to much writing. Debarred by his ill health, and frequently by the weakness of his voice, from many opportunities of personal intercourse, he often expressed in writing the sentiments which he would otherwise have spoken; and with as much freedom and ease as most people could converse. His celebrity as an author, and as a man of benevolence, induced many persons, even strangers, to write to him, soliciting advice, or pecuniary assistance: to all these letters he seldom failed to return prompt and kind answers. His letters of consolation and congratulation, in particular, were numerous: for so lively was the interest which he took in the affairs of those persons, with whom he was connected or acquainted, that occasions of sorrow or joy seldom occurred to them, or in their families, which did not call forth from him an expression of tender and pious sympathy. His letters were not designed, nor, as he observed, calculated for the public, but exclusively for the persons to whom they were addressed: he has, therefore, as I have mentioned in the preface, left in writing a request that they may not be published. To all his correspondents, whose feeling and delicacy are, in any degree, congenial to his own, they will, from that very circumstance, become the more deeply interesting, and the more valuable, not, indeed, in a pecuniary point of view, but intrinsically; and they will, I doubt not, be preserved with reverential care, as precious relics of a departed friend and monitor.

As a neighbour, Mr. Murray was highly respected, and truly exemplary. He was solicitous to avoid either giving or taking offence; loath to believe, and still more loath to propagate, any idle tales, or rumours, or to make any censorious remarks; ready to unite, as far as his situation would allow, in every useful plan for general accommodation, or advantage;* unwilling to interfere in other people's affairs, or to offer his advice, unless he thought it would be acceptable or beneficial; and very humane and liberal to the poor, particularly in time of sickness. During the greater part of his abode in England, he was not able to associate much with his neigh-

* Amongst numerous instances of this kind, the following, though comparatively small, is characteristic, and therefore, not unworthy of notice. Unable to walk himself, he contributed largely towards forming and keeping up a walk, by the side of the road, leading from Holdgate and other places, to the city of York. A seat, on which to rest the weary traveller, was put up, by the side of this walk, entirely at Mr. Murray's own expense: which, it is to be hoped, will not be injured or demolished by rude, rapacious hands; but will henceforth be called Murray's seat, and preserved as a humble memorial of a great and good man, who lived near the spot where it is placed, and who, by his long residence, has given celebrity to the little village of Holdgate, and its environs.

bours: but scarcely any one ever resided in his immediate vicinity, who did not, in some way or other, receive from him, some kind, delicate, attention, or some essential service. Both himself and his wife seemed not only to embrace, but to contrive, opportunities of serving and obliging.

Mr. Murray preserved an habitual tenderness of mind. He loved to be at peace with all persons, especially those with whom he was most conversant. He seemed grieved whenever he perceived, that, through inadvertence, or any unavoidable circumstance, he had given pain, or the slightest cause of offence, to any one; and always wished for, and gladly embraced, an early opportunity of endeavouring to remove the impression.

On all occasions of provocation occurring to himself, particularly when he received any mark of inattention, unkindness, or even ingratitude, from those to whom he was attached, or whom he had served, he evidently felt keenly; but he never expressed any sentiment, or uttered any expression, unbecoming a Christian. His emotion soon subsided; and his resentment passed away, quick as a transient cloud on a fine summer's day. Not only the sun never went down on his anger; but even the next hour scarcely saw any traces of it. On many occasions, he has been known, to take the earliest opportunity of renewing his civility, to those persons by whom his feelings had been thus tried, or of conferring fresh favours upon them: thus, not encouraging evil, but endeavouring, according to the Scripture maxim, to overcome evil with good.

He was full of candour, and Christian charity. Though far removed from that weak credulity which is imposed on by every plausible pretence, or artful profession, he certainly appeared quicker in discerning good than evil, in human character and conduct; or, at least, he pointed it out, and commented upon it, with greater alacrity. The good was pleasant to him, and congenial to his feelings. The ill he passed by as lightly as circumstances would allow. He condemned with regret; and readily admitted every extenuation.

He was pleased with little services and attentions, and grateful for them. He was ready to oblige, and willing to be obliged. To confer favours was pleasant to him: he could not, therefore, refuse to others, in their turn, the gratification which he so often felt. A gift, or mark of attention, however small, however awkwardly presented, when offered by those whom he had obliged, seldom failed to be received by him in the most gracious manner. On such occasions, he would sometimes say: "This person thinks himself indebted to me; he wishes to discharge part of the debt, or, at least, to make some acknowledgment of it: why should I, by my refusal, or cold acceptance, deny him this gratification?"

In the performance of relative duties, Mr. Murray did not forget humanity to animals; of which the following is a striking instance, amongst many others that might be given. In early life, he was fond of shooting; but after some years he became dissatisfied with it, from a conviction, not only that it consumes too much precious time, but also that it is improper to take away life for the sake of amusement. He believed that of the birds which are shot at, many more are wounded, than are actually killed and obtained; and, consequently, they gradually pine away, and die through pain, and want of food. He had seen birds so much hurt, as to be incapable of performing their natural functions; and he had reason to believe that instances of this kind are very numerous. These reflections made such an impression on his mind, that he determined never again to indulge himself in a sport, which produced so much distress to the objects of his amusement.

He was a true patriot. America, his native land, the abode of his relations, and his own, during a great part of his life, was dear to him:

England also was dear to him; it was his adopted country, and the scene of his greatest usefulness. He rejoiced in the prosperity of both countries; and particularly wished that peace and amity should prevail between them. He was a friend of liberty, both civil and religious; a warm assertor of the just rights of man, and averse to despotic power, whether lodged in the hands of one, or of many: but, at the same time, he was a friend of order, a strenuous supporter of good government, and opposed to all wild theories and useless innovation. The British constitution he much admired: "a fabric," as he observes in one of his publications, "which has stood the test of ages, and attracted the admiration of the world. It combines the advantages of the three great forms of government, without their inconveniences: it preserves a happy balance amongst them: and it contains within itself, the power of recurring to first principles, and of rectifying all the disorders of time."

Mr. Murray was a philanthropist in the justest and most extensive sense of the word. His benevolence was not confined to any nation, sect, or party. It took in the whole human race, of every clime and colour. Springing from a principle of duty and of love to God and his creatures, it did not exhaust itself in mere sentiment or feeling; but diffused its benign influence over his character and conduct. He promoted, by all the means in his power, the welfare and improvement of mankind. He took a deep interest in the success of various public institutions, designed to serve the cause of religion and humanity, particularly the Bible society and the African institution; and he contributed largely according to his means, though sometimes anonymously, to their support. By his writings, by his life and conversation, by the encouragement which he gave not only to public but to private endeavours, of a benevolent and religious nature, he promoted, in an eminent degree, the general diffusion of the spirit of Christianity. The good seed which was intrusted to his care, he cast upon a wide extent of land: the abundant harvest which it has produced, and which, I trust, it will long continue to produce, will, probably, be fully made known to him in the world to come.

His acts of private charity were innumerable: indeed, many of them were known only to himself and his wife, and to those who were the immediate objects of them. All his favours were rendered doubly acceptable even to the poorest persons, by the civility, kindness, or tenderness, with which they were bestowed. The profit which he derived from his various publications, was uniformly devoted to benevolent purposes, and afforded him a considerable fund of charity. But long before he received any assistance from this source, he was distinguished by his beneficence: he gave much alms; he distributed books of piety; and he contributed, in various ways, to render more comfortable many persons in straitened circumstances. From the commencement of his residence at Holdgate, till his decease, he paid, annually, for the schooling of several poor children in his neighbourhood; which, before the general establishment of Sunday and other schools, was a peculiarly acceptable and useful charity.

By his great abilities and application, and his respectable family connexions, he had, through the blessing of Providence, acquired, early in life, a portion of this world's goods more than adequate to his own moderate wants and wishes, and those of his wife: the overplus he devoted to the service of God and man. Nay, I think it may be said, he dedicated all he had to the Lord; his fortune, his time, his talents. His house was the seat of simplicity, piety, and benevolence. It was abundantly supplied with every thing necessary for the comfortable accommodation of its inhabitants, and of visiters; but there was nothing for show, or mere ornament. From taste, as well as principle, Mr. Murray was averse to an ostentatious or luxurious mode of living.

His income, independently of the profit of his publications, scarcely at any time exceeded five or six hundred pounds a year. With this income, he was hospitable and generous: he lived in a plain way indeed, but so respectably, and with so high a character for benevolence, that he was generally esteemed rich.—He frequently acknowledged as one of the blessings of Providence, that from his first establishment in life, he had always had the means of living with comfort and respectability.

His external manners were truly pleasing. He was affable and courteous in his address; mild, yet dignified, in his demeanour. His unaffected civility and kindness readily won their way to the heart. Though a valetudinarian during the greater part of his life, his personal habits were those of uncommon delicacy and decorum.

His appearance was noble and prepossessing. He was tall, and well proportioned; and rather stout. His complexion was dark: it did not exhibit that sickly appearance which might have been expected from his general debility, and long confinement. His forehead was open, expansive, and rather elevated. His features were regular. The profile of his face, if not handsome, was strikingly noble and pleasing. The general impression of his countenance indicated at once the elevation of his mind, and the sweetness of his disposition. When he received and welcomed any stranger, or visiter, for whom he felt particular respect or regard, his countenance beamed with increased dignity and sweetness; his eyes sparkled with benevolent animation, and a smile played on his lips: his whole appearance and manner, bespoke instantaneously and powerfully, superior intelligence sweetly tempered by superior goodness and benignity. The effect produced on the mind of the beholder, though often felt, can scarcely be described: it was a mingled sensation of admiration, love, and reverence. Some have said, after their first introduction to him, that his aspect and demeanour, together with the purity and sanctity of his character, recalled to their minds the idea of the apostles and other holy men; who, in the early ages of Christianity, were, with a large measure of grace, redeemed from the world, and dedicated to the service of God and religion.

CHAPTER III.

REMARKS ON THE AUTHOR'S VARIOUS PUBLICATIONS.

BEING well acquainted with the publications of Mr. Murray, and having had peculiar opportunities of knowing their merits, and the views of the author, I presume that a few remarks on them, both general and particular, will not be unacceptable to the reader. They are a tribute which seems due to my departed friend, for his meritorious exertions to advance the interests of religion and literature; and they may be the means of attracting attention to some excellences of design or execution, which might otherwise have been passed over unobserved, or with less consideration than they deserve.

It is a striking recommendation of these works, that they have had a considerable influence, in promoting the correct and chaste education of young persons. The strain of piety and virtue, and the elegant taste, which pervade them, have had happy effects, in forming the minds of young persons who have studied them; and in producing, or expanding, a similar spirit, in the publications since introduced into seminaries. The author was very strongly impressed with the importance of a guarded education of youth: and he thought that if sound principles of piety and virtue, were constantly presented to them, and happily incorporated with the elements of literature, the effect would be incalculably greater than most persons are apt to imagine. This sentiment induced him to believe, that he could not better employ his time, or render a greater service to society, than by composing works of education, in which learning and knowledge should go hand in hand with moral and religious instruction. This design he has most successfully accomplished: and the universal approbation which it has obtained, is a very pleasing proof of the importance and usefulness of his writings. He had great satisfaction in reflecting on the moral effects which his works are calculated to produce; and that none of them contains a sentiment capable of giving him pain in the retrospect of life.—He has, I trust, planted, and he will continue to plant, in the minds of a long succession of young readers and students, principles and virtues, which will support and animate them in every period of this life; and which may, indeed, have a great influence on their happiness in another world.

Mr. Murray's grammatical works possess distinguished merit, both as to matter and arrangement. He has introduced into this branch of science great simplicity and perspicuity. And since these works have appeared, a subject which was before generally considered as dry and uninteresting, to young persons especially, has become very popular, and is now almost universally studied and relished. To render our native tongue an object of peculiar attention; to excite a general desire to acquire the knowledge of it; and to facilitate that acquisition; reflect not a little credit on the productions of our author.

It is an additional recommendation of his publications, that they all have the same objects in view, are intimately connected, and naturally introduce one another. The subsequent works generally illustrate and enforce the principles of those which precede. To instil into the youthful mind the love of piety and virtue; to infuse into it sentiments of importance on topics of an interesting nature; and to excite a taste for judicious composition, and a correct and elegant style; are the objects which are constantly aimed at, in all these literary productions. They may, therefore, be properly considered as forming a little code of important elementary instruction, adapted to the varied years and capacities of young persons; and may, with confidence, be put into their hands.

It may not be improper to observe, that our author has been of considerable use too, in promoting the printing of works of education, with accuracy and neatness; on good paper, with a clear type, and in a fair, open manner. All his publications, from the first to the last of them, have appeared in this very proper and attractive form.* He thought it was of no small importance in the business of education; and his practice, in this respect, has been successfully imitated.

His publications are entitled to commendatory notice, on account of their negative as well as their positive merit. Indeed, their freedom from every thing objectionable, constitutes one of their most solid recommendations. There is in them no expression or sentiment of an indelicate nature; nothing which tends to vitiate taste, or undermine principle; nothing that is vulgar or frivolous, eccentric or dubious; nor is there, on the other hand, any thing too nice, critical, or refined, for general use and acceptance. Mr.

* It must, in justice, be observed, that the typography of Mr. Murray's works, reflects credit, not only on the author, but on the printers, Messrs. Wilson and Co. of York; who are also publishers, and, in part, proprietors of these works. Their extensive printing establishment, only about a mile distant from the residence of Mr. Murray; the ability, promptitude, and obligingness, with which they promoted his views; were particularly satisfactory to him, and afforded him great facility and accommodation, in the ordering and managing of his various publications.

Murray aims at nothing which he does not accomplish; nor does he aim at any thing, which is not worth accomplishing. His books are a considerable and an acknowledged improvement on all existing works of the same nature. He does not pursue ideal or imaginary perfection; he accommodates his works to the tastes and capacities of young persons, for whom they are chiefly designed, and to the present state of society and of literature.

The Christian Observer, in noticing his octavo Grammar, says: "We are happy to bear testimony that none of the sentences and extracts appear to be selected with relation to the peculiar creed of the writer." With equal truth it may be said, that our author's other publications are clear of any expressions or sentiments, peculiar to the society of which he was a member. He made it a point, whilst he was writing for the benefit of readers in general, to avoid introducing, in any shape, the tenets of a particular sect; or any thing which could be supposed to relate to those tenets. And for this judicious care and liberality, he has been much and deservedly commended. At the same time, it must be observed that he avoided introducing any thing inconsistent with, or contrary to, the tenets of the sect to which he belonged; so that, whilst his works have received the approbation of the public in general, they have been no less highly appreciated by the members of his own society.

The preceding observations on Mr. Murray's works, are supported and confirmed by the opinions of the public critics, and of various other writers. A statement of some of these opinions may not improperly be adduced on the present occasion.

The British Critic contains the following remarks: "Our pages bear ample testimony, both to the ability and the diligence of Mr. Murray. His different publications evince much sound judgment and good sense; and his Selections are very well calculated to answer the intended purpose."

"This author," says the Christian Observer, "deserves much praise and encouragement for the pains he has taken in purifying books of instruction; and his English Grammar will establish his character as a writer in this important department of literature."

The Eclectic Review observes, that "Mr. Murray's exertions are directed to one of the noblest objects. They are judicious, unremitted, and, we rejoice to add, particularly acceptable to the public. His works are distinguished from the mass of school books, by a correct style, a refined taste, and especially by a vigilant subservience to morality and religion."

The Anti-jacobin Review gives the following very ample recommendation: "The principle upon which all the publications of Mr. Murray, for the instruction of the rising generation are founded, is such as gives him an unquestionable claim to public protection. The man who blends religion and morals with the elements of scientific knowledge, renders an eminent service to society; and where ability of execution is added to excellence of design, as in the present case, the claim becomes irresistible."

In the American Review and Literary Journal is the following eulogium on Mr. Murray's works: "Mr. Murray's Grammar, as well as his other publications, has received the uniform approbation of literary characters and journalists. We do not hesitate warmly to recommend them to the instructers of youth in every part of the United States, as eminently conducive to pure morality and religion, and to the acquisition of a correct and elegant style. They deserve to take place of all other works of the same kind."

Dr. Miller, in his "Retrospect of the Eighteenth Century," observes that "Mr. Lindley Murray, by his English Grammar, and by several other publications connected with it, and designed as auxiliaries to its principal purpose, has become entitled to the gratitude of every friend to English literature, and to true virtue."

Mr. Walker, author of a judicious and highly approved Pronouncing Dictionary, and of various other works, has, in his "Elements of Elocution," and in his "Outlines of English Grammar," borne a very striking testimony to the merits of our author. "Mr. Murray's Grammar, and Selection of lessons for reading, are the best in the English language."—"I need not acquaint the public with the merit and success of Lindley Murray's Grammar; which seems to have superseded every other. Indeed, when we consider the plain, simple mode of instruction he has adopted; the extent of observation he has displayed; and the copious variety of illustration he has added; we shall not wonder that his Grammar has been so universally applauded."

The letters which Mr. Murray received, at an early period of the publication of his works, from a celebrated writer on education, and on other important subjects, contain the following passages: "You appear to have simplified Grammar beyond any of your precursors. I am also better pleased with your English Reader, than with any compilation I have ever seen.—I am happy to see you so carefully guarding the elements of literature, and fencing off the obtrusion of any immoral author, or corrupt sentiment."—"We are both, I trust, co-operators in the same great cause, that of impressing young minds with right principles, as well as keeping out of their way, what would serve only to corrupt and deprave them. Preoccupying the ground, by safe, early instruction, of various kinds, and supplying, in some measure, their early literary wants, you, I trust, will be enabled so far to form their minds to virtue and religion, that they will reject from taste, as well as avoid from principle, the destructive, and also the vain and idle compositions, to which so much youthful time is unthinkingly sacrificed.—I never neglect an opportunity, when it is fairly offered, of bearing my testimony to your works; and I have never heard them named by any one into whose hands they have fallen, but with respect and approbation. They will, I doubt not, more and more make their way; and, as they are more known, will be generally adopted."

Another highly respectable writer on education, expresses himself in a letter to our author, in the following terms: "You must allow me to observe, that no man, who feels as an Englishman or a Christian, can contemplate, without the highest satisfaction, the very extensive circulation which your works have obtained. It is books of this description, which the last chapter of my Essay was designed to recommend to our schools: and I still think, that on the use or neglect of them, depend, in no small degree, the principles of the rising generation, and consequently our permanence and prosperity as a nation."

A letter to Mr. Murray from the president of one of the American colleges, contains the following sentiments: "Your grammatical works have always been esteemed by me, as the most valuable yet published; and hence, I have never ceased to recommend the careful study of them to the youth of this college. The advantage which both students and scholars have derived from such a study, has been great. The knowledge, and the proper use, of our own language, have become an indispensable acquirement; and with the lights which you have held forth, that valuable acquirement is accessible to every one. Too long had the study of our own language yielded to that of Latin and Greek, or of some modern language. You have the merit of producing a reform in this respect; for which every friend of literature owes to you the greatest obligation."

A distinguished and elegant author, having occasion to write to Mr. Murray, on a subject unconnected with his works, embraced the opportunity of expressing his opinion respecting them. "I cannot," says he, "deny myself the pleasure of offering you, upon this occasion, my best thanks, as a part of the public, for the many judicious and truly valuable works, with which you have enriched our language. The rising generation, and those who are concerned in their superintendence, are greatly your debtors: and, if to have been made useful, under God, in promoting sound learning, pure religion, and liberal sentiments, be (as it certainly is) a ground of satisfactory reflection, you are entitled to that enjoyment, in no ordinary degree."

I shall only add an extract from another letter to Mr. Murray, on the subject of his works. It was written by a respectable and learned clergyman, with whom he had been acquainted in early life. "After your performances have passed the ordeal of public criticism, and received the approbation of all the British and American Reviews, it would be presumption in me to give an opinion, or to add my feeble voice to the common plaudit. Indeed, I do not recollect any publications, that have so entirely escaped censure, and so universally obtained commendation. I rejoice much in their extensive circulation, because they will not only improve the rising generation, in the knowledge of grammar, and in correct reading, writing, and composition; but strongly impress on their tender minds the principles of morality and religion, and make them not only better scholars, but better men. If generally introduced (as they will be) into our public schools and seminaries, they will counteract the baneful effects of some late licentious productions; and furnish youth with an armour, which will imbolden and enable them to repel, through life, the weapons of vice and infidelity."

Having made these general observations on the works of Mr. Murray, I proceed to consider their merits individually.

The first of his publications was, the POWER of RELIGION on the MIND.

This work, as he often observed, afforded him the most heartfelt satisfaction. Though it has not procured him the most literary reputation, it was his favourite performance. It was viewed by him in this light, because he conceived that it was more immediately adapted than any of his other works, to lead the readers to a virtuous and happy life; and to excite in them an ardent desire, and earnest preparation, for that state of eternal felicity which is the great end of their being. On his own mind, the lives of good men, and the efficacy of religion in the closing scene of life, had made a happy impression. The elevated hopes and lively faith of pious persons, in their dying moments, who are just entering into the regions of glory, where all their virtuous conflicts will be infinitely overpaid, are, indeed, of the most consoling and animating nature. They strengthen confidence in religion; and encourage perseverance in its paths. That the author of this book should be desirous of exciting in the breasts of others, the encouragements to piety and virtue, which he had himself felt from contemplating exalted goodness, was natural and laudable; and he has, in consequence, produced a valuable work, which has been much read, and highly commended. Besides the proof of approbation, which the sale of seventeen editions, some of them consisting of three or four thousand copies, has afforded, the author received very gratifying information of several individuals who had been excited to virtue, or strengthened in a religious course of life, by the perusal of this publication. From many persons of piety and learning, he also received letters, which expressed, in strong terms, their approbation of the performance; and their opinion that it is happily calculated to counteract the growing spirit of infidelity and irreligion.

The work is, in every point of view, well executed. The subjects have been judiciously selected from the mass of biography, consisting generally of distinguished individuals of different periods, countries, and professions; whose sentiments would probably be listened to with reverence. An historical sketch of each person is given, sufficient to make the reader acquainted with him, and to give an interest to his testimony on behalf of religion. This individual testimony does not embrace a great number and variety of expressions, which might be tedious to many readers: it is confined to a few striking and important declarations. And yet the sentiments of each person, when united together, form a considerable body of religious instruction, copiously varied, and communicated in the most weighty and impressive manner. The facts stated in the work are well authenticated; the arrangement is judicious; and the language is simple and correct.

In characterizing this little volume, the Monthly Reviewers, with great propriety, observe, that "Mr. Murray has furnished an interesting collection of testimonies; and we wonder not, that a work so instructive and amusing, as well as impressive, should have been generally patronised. It is a book which may be read, with profit, by persons in all situations." —The Guardian of Education also speaks in high terms of the publication: "This work, in its present enlarged state, forms, in our opinion, one of the best books that can be put into the hands of young people. The subject is grave and important; but Mr. Murray has rendered it highly interesting and engaging, by a judicious selection of anecdotes and examples; which, by the intermixture of pious reflections, he teaches the reader to apply to his own benefit."

Mr. Murray considered the extensive circulation of this work, and the very general approbation which it has received, as a pleasing evidence, that a regard for piety and virtue, for true practical religion, is sincere and lively; and prevails in a much greater degree, than some gloomy and unfavourable circumstances would induce us, at the first view, to suppose.—The success of this performance, and the good which it was the means of producing, were considerations of the most soothing nature to the heart of the author; and excited his gratitude to God, that he had been made of some use in promoting the best interests of mankind.

The next work which Mr. Murray presented to the public, was his ENGLISH GRAMMAR.

This is a performance of distinguished merit. "It shows," as one of his literary correspondents justly observes, "an extensive knowledge of the subject; and, what is seldom joined with it, a judicious distinction between the speculative and the practical, the curious and the useful parts of grammar."

The author has modestly called this work a compilation. But the critical and attentive reader of it knows, that besides its great improvement in the arrangement of the various subjects, and the logical division of its parts, it contains many highly ingenious positions that are perfectly original. In particular, the discussions, which are dispersed through the book, and intended to illustrate and support the author's grammatical system in general, as well as to defend some special points; will be allowed to be not only new, but to contain much acute and satisfactory reasoning. His views of the cases of English nouns, and the moods and tenses of our verbs, are so judicious, and so consonant with the nature and idiom of our language, that teachers almost universally acquiesce in the propriety of his arrangements.

The definitions and the rules throughout the Grammar, are expressed with neatness and perspicuity. They are as short and comprehensive as the nature of the subject would admit: and they are well adapted both to the understanding and the memory of young persons. The mode of parsing which our author recommends, is admirably calculated to confirm and perfect the scholar in what he has previously learned; and to enable him thoroughly to understand, and readily to apply, the rules, both principal and subordinate.

It may truly be said, that the language in every part of the work, is simple, correct, and perspicuous; and, consequently, well calculated to improve the taste and habits of the student, in the cultivation of his native tongue. In an elementary work, it is of consequence that no awkward or vulgar expressions, no harsh or irregular constructions, should occur. In the Grammar, at present under review, the reverse of all these imperfections, is very conspicuous.

A particular recommendation of this Grammar, is, that it embraces all the parts of the science; and gives to each of them that attention which its relative importance demands. The student, by this means, surveys the whole of his subject; and derives the advantage which results from such a connected view, at the same time that he is not detained, nor disgusted, by too prolix a discussion of any particular part. The author has, with great propriety, distinguished by a larger letter, all the rules and observations which are of primary importance; and, by this means, a judicious outline, or general view, of the more prominent parts of the subject, is happily presented to the student. When this comprehensive view has been taken, the subordinate points, contained in the smaller type, will be perused to the greatest advantage. Many of these explain the principles, on which the rules and positions are founded; showing their origin to be in the constitution of the human mind, or in the reason and nature of things: and, so far as these explanations extend, they may properly be said to exhibit the philosophy of grammar. This work is also valuable, for its occasional references to the various opinions of other English grammarians; and for the comparisons which it often institutes, on particular points, between the English and other languages. And yet the author has studiously avoided every thing that tends to involve in obscurity, the subjects on which he treats. His system is connected and uniform; his plan and materials are such as are adapted to the present structure of the language; and his reasonings are calculated to preserve its regularity, and prevent useless and unwarrantable innovations. In these points of view, this Grammar is entitled to high estimation. An approved and established system of grammatical rules and principles, judiciously expressed and arranged, according to which the youth of our country are educated, and which may serve as a general standard of rectitude on these subjects, is certainly a great and national benefit; and entitles the author to the respect and gratitude of the literary world.

The Appendix to the Grammar is introduced with peculiar propriety. The learner, by his preceding acquirements, is fully prepared to enter upon this part of the work. It will not only confirm the rules of construction which he has already learned; but, by regular transitions, it will lead him forward to the principles and practice of perspicuous and elegant composition. The rules for attaining purity, propriety, and precision of language, both with regard to single words and phrases, and the construction of sentences, are exhibited with great order and judgment; and illustrated by a variety of examples which clearly show the importance and usefulness of the rules. This Appendix is, I believe, generally allowed to contain, in a small compass, a greater number of excellent rules and principles, with happy illustrations, for teaching accurate and elegant composition, than is to be found in any other publication.

The Grammar is closed by a sensible, affectionate, and truly Christian "Address to young students," on the proper application of their literary attainments, and the happiness they would find in a pious and virtuous course of life. This short address, especially with the last additions to it, contains many excellent sentiments and admonitions; and it is expressed in a style and manner well adapted to make serious and lasting impressions on the minds of youth. It is fraught with just and elevated views of learning and religion: and the solicitude of the author, that the young persons whom he addresses, may answer the great end of their existence, both here and hereafter, can scarcely fail of disposing their minds to listen with reverence to his affectionate recommendations. This address will, I doubt not, be read by many young students with a lively interest; and confirm or awaken in them an attachment to the cause of religion and virtue.

Mr. Murray's Grammar being so celebrated a work, and so extensively circulated, a more particular account of the occasion of his writing it, than is given in his Memoirs, may not be unacceptable to the reader. Some of his friends established, at York, a school for the guarded education of young females; which was continued for several years. Mr. Murray strongly recommended that the study of the English language, should form a prominent part of instruction. The young persons employed as the first teachers, not being sufficiently qualified in this respect, he kindly undertook to instruct them at his own house; and, for their use, he made some extracts from Blair, Campbell, and other writers, which afterwards formed the basis of the Appendix to his English Grammar. By these young teachers, he was much importuned to write an English Grammar, for the benefit of their pupils, on the same plan of simplicity, clearness, and regular gradation, which he had pursued in his verbal instructions. Their requests were sanctioned and enforced, by the superintendents of the school, and by some of his other friends: he was at length induced to comply. In preparing the work, and consenting to its publication, he had no expectation that it would be used, except by the school for which it was designed, and two or three other schools, conducted by persons who were also his friends.

Such was the humble origin of his Grammar; which I have often heard him mention, even amongst literary persons, with great humility, simplicity, and candour. The first public recommendations of the work which he read, gave him the most lively joy, accompanied by some degree of surprise. The success of the Grammar naturally led to the publication of other works, in which general benefit and extensive circulation were contemplated. The occasion of his writing the "Power of Religion," is mentioned in his Memoirs. It was designed merely for his own distribution amongst his friends and neighbours. Thus his commencing author, did not arise from any overweening conceit of his own abilities, nor from any desire of literary fame, or even any idea that he could attain it; but from a disinterested and unfeigned desire to do good, in a small circle; to disseminate useful knowledge, correct literary taste, and above all, moral and religious principles.—I have often thought that no part of his life is more exemplary, or striking, than the great humility, and earnest desire to do good, with which he began, and indeed continued, his literary career; and that the eminent success which attended his labours, may, without presumption or superstition, be attributed, in great measure, to the blessing of Providence on motives of action so pure, so pious and benevolent.—The excellence of his character contributed also in no small degree to the success of his works: his kindness made him many friends, who were anxious, from regard to him, to receive and circulate them; and a general impression very justly prevailed, that whatever proceeded from him would be distinguished by good sense, good taste, correct language, and the soundest principles of religion and morality.

The next works which were published by Mr. Murray, were his English Exercises and Key.

The Grammar exhibits the principles and rules of the language: these works contain most copious examples and illustrations of the rules; and display them in almost every possible variety. They give more extended views of each subject than are found in the Grammar, or could conveniently have been there introduced. The great diversity of these illustrations serves also, in many instances, as substitutes for a considerable number of minute subordinate rules, which it would have been tedious to have drawn out into regular form.

It is not unusual to exhibit grammatical English exercises, in the most coarse and vulgar manner. The errors are so glaring, that learners can scarcely commit them; and they are often so extremely awkward, that the proper words and construction cannot easily be discovered. They are, in short, more calculated to puzzle and mislead the learner, than to afford him any instruction. The author of these Exercises has greatly served the cause of education, by the judicious manner in which they are executed. Both teachers and pupils are under no small obligation to him for these labours. No errors are admitted into his Exercises, but such as are commonly to be met with in respectable writings and conversation: and, for this reason, the Key which corrects the erroneous constructions, will render these books of great use to all persons, who wish to express themselves in accurate and unexceptionable terms. Some parts of the Exercises and Key are indeed adapted to young learners; but many other parts of them are calculated for the improvement of persons, who have made considerable proficiency in the study of the language. These books have consequently been found well adapted to inculcate and exemplify the refinements and peculiarities of the English tongue. They possess great merit; and it may justly be said of them, in the words of the Monthly Review, that, "they occupy, with distinguished excellence, a most important place in the science of the English language; and may be warmly recommended to the teachers of schools, as well as to all those who are desirous of attaining correctness and precision in their native tongue."

A peculiar advantage of these Exercises, is, that they consist almost altogether of sentences which inculcate important sentiments respecting morality, religion, and civil life: all of which, as exhibited in the Key, are expressed in the most correct, perspicuous, and easy language. The author was studious to select illustrations of this nature; and, by this means, to combine every advantage of which the subject is capable. It is unnecessary to enlarge on the benefits, which Exercises so constructed must produce to the learner, with regard to expression, taste, and composition.

These Exercises furnish to the student a very pleasing mode of improving himself in the construction of our language. In surveying the inaccurate sentence, his ingenuity is exercised in correcting every part which he thinks requires amendment: and on a reference to the Key, he has the satisfaction of perceiving that he had made the corrections properly, or of knowing the points in which he had failed, and of being guarded, in future, against errors of a similar nature. And he is confirmed in the propriety of these corrections, by turning to the rules in the Grammar, on which they are founded. Improvement thus acquired, is not only peculiarly gratifying to an ingenious mind, but must be impressive and permanent.

About the time that the Exercises and Key appeared, our author published an ABRIDGMENT of his Grammar.

This is a very neat and judicious little work. It is calculated for two purposes: first, to convey a competent knowledge of grammar to those who are not designed to make an extensive progress in the study; and secondly, to serve as an Introduction to the author's larger Grammar, in those schools where both the books are used. The utility of this work has been abundantly evinced, by the very extensive sale which it has had. In this country, about forty-eight thousand copies have been annually sold for many years past; and I believe that the number of copies sold, from the first publication of the work to the present time, amounts to one million.

Our author's three volumes of the ENGLISH READER, and the INTRODUCTION and SEQUEL to it, have met with high approbation from the public. The design and execution of these volumes are truly excellent; and well adapted to promote their professed objects, improvement in the art of reading, and storing the youthful mind with the finest moral and religious sentiments. These sentiments possess the additional merit of being so happily diversified, as to comprise a great body of instruction most important to young persons. As the pieces which form these volumes, are taken from the best English writers, the composition is, of course, correct, and the language finished and elegant. The benefit which young students will reap from the perusal of such models of excellence, early and impressively set before them, cannot be duly appreciated but by those who have had the best opportunities to reflect on the subject. The compiler has selected, with the utmost care, what he conceived to be particularly adapted to engage the youthful mind, and to present to it the most amiable and striking views of piety and virtue. He has too embraced every suitable occasion to exhibit the Christian religion in the most attractive form; and to recommend to the serious attention of young persons its divine and deeply interesting doctrines and precepts.—I shall close the observations on these three volumes, by a short extract from the Monthly Review. "We recommend this small volume (the English Reader) to those who wish to attain, without the help of instructers, the important advantages of thinking and speaking with propriety.—We have no doubt that the public will be pleased with the additions (the Introduction and Sequel) to both the fronts of the original building. The whole is truly useful, and well arranged. Displaying a sound judgment, and actuated by the purest motives, this gentleman is indeed entitled to the fullest praise."

Our author's two French publications, the INTRODUCTION AU LECTEUR FRANÇOIS and the LECTEUR FRANÇOIS, are highly worthy of commendation. They are, in a peculiar manner, acceptable to parents and teachers, who are desirous that their children and pupils should acquire a knowledge of the French language, without imbibing a spirit of frivolity, or lax principles of morality. Chaste, correct, and elegant, these works exhibit fine specimens of the language; and instruct the learner, by the easiest gradations, in the various styles of the best French writers. The "Preliminary Rules and Observations," in the "Introduction au Lecteur François," and the

Appendix to that work, are well calculated to facilitate the acquisition of the French language; and that not in a superficial manner, but radically. The selections in both volumes are of the choicest nature; and forcibly inculcate sound morality and religion, adorned with all the graces of language and composition. The "Lecteur François," in particular, is a truly classical work; and it will, doubtless, be long read and admired by persons who have a taste for French literature, or who are desirous of improving themselves in the language. Correctness and accuracy in the printing of books designed to teach a foreign language, are highly desirable, and indeed indispensable. This advantage the works in question possess in no ordinary degree; both with respect to orthography and accentuation.

The English Spelling-Book composed by our author, though it is a small volume, is a work which bears the marks of great judgment and ingenuity; and, perhaps, it is not inferior in point of ability and literary execution, to any of his publications. The gradation throughout the work is easy and regular; and well adapted to the progress of the infant understanding. The advances from letters to syllables, from syllables to words, and from words to sentences, are carried on by almost insensible degrees. The first lessons of spelling are of the simplest nature, and they imperceptibly slide into those which follow: the reading lessons are so carefully adjusted as to contain no words, which the scholar has not previously spelled. The sections of spelling are constructed and arranged in such a manner, as to afford great assistance in acquiring the true pronunciation both of letters and words. The division of syllables which the author has adopted, and his rules for spelling, are consonant to the best authorities, and to the analogy of the language. The more advanced reading lessons are admirably calculated to attract and interest young readers; as well as to impress their minds with moral and religious sentiments, suited to their age and capacity. Under a garb of great simplicity, these lessons convey an uncommon portion of instruction, adapted to children in all ranks of life.

In the plan and execution of this work, the reader who is skilled in the subject, will find considerable originality, of a truly useful nature. And I believe, that the more accurately this little volume is examined, the more it will be approved. One of Mr. Murray's literary correspondents speaks of it in the following terms: "It surpasses every elementary work of the kind, in felicity of arrangement, and in perspicuity, comprehensiveness, and accuracy of information."

The First Book for Children, was published at the same time as the Spelling-Book. It consists, chiefly, of the most easy and simple parts of that work; with some additional reading lessons. It has been justly characterized as a "very improved primer."

The next publication of our author, was his English Grammar, in two volumes octavo.

It comprises the Grammar, Exercises, and Key, united in one connected and uniform system. The first volume contains the principles and rules of the language, which are amply and most judiciously exemplified in the second volume. These exemplifications are of so great importance to the clear comprehension of the rules, that the work would have been very defective without them. The two volumes, in their present state, are generally acknowledged to constitute the best system of English grammar, which has hitherto appeared. When this new form of our author's grammatical works was contemplated, he thought it afforded a proper occasion, for extending and improving some of the principles and positions contained in the duodecimo Grammar; and he has done this very amply, and doubtless, much to the satisfaction of those who possess a critical knowledge of the subject. Of this work the public critics have given a highly favourable character. "The

"Christian Observers," in particular, speak of it, as "a work of great correctness and perfection;" and recommend it to teachers, to foreigners, and to young persons who have left school. A distinguished author, in a letter addressed to Mr. Murray, expresses the following sentiments respecting this publication: "I have great satisfaction in congratulating you on the completion of your system of English Grammar. The British and American nations owe you a high obligation, for the service you have rendered to English literature, by your learned and elaborate work. You may safely anticipate the gratitude of a long succession of students of English Grammar, in both hemispheres; and of writers in the English language, who will recur to your work as a standard in settling the principles, and adjusting the niceties, of composition."—The work has already gone through five editions in this country; and it has been frequently reprinted in America.

In contemplating the different publications of Mr. Murray, on grammar, it is peculiarly satisfactory to observe, how happily he has provided every class of students with the means of acquiring a knowledge of their native language. The Abridgment is calculated for the minor schools, and for those who use it as introductory to the larger work. The duodecimo Grammar, and the

Exercises and Key, are suited to academies, and to private learners. The octavo edition claims the attention of persons, who aim at higher attainments in the language; who wish for an extensive and critical knowledge of the subject. To many it will serve as a book of reference; in ascertaining what is proper, and correcting what is erroneous, in English composition. Both as an elegant and a scientific work, it will, I doubt not, find a place in the libraries of all persons, who are desirous of understanding the construction of their native tongue, and of speaking and writing it with accuracy and perspicuity; or who wish to encourage and patronise the literature of their country.

The "Selection from Bishop Horne's Commentary on the Psalms," and "The Duty and Benefit of a Daily Perusal of the Holy Scriptures," having been spoken of in a preceding chapter, no further mention of them seems requisite.

It will probably be satisfactory to the reader, to be informed of the prices which Mr. Murray received for the copyrights of his different works; I shall, therefore, present him with an accurate statement. Though inadequate to the subsequent success of the works, they were certainly very liberal at the time they were given; and, I believe, greater than ever had been given for works of a similar nature. The sale of most of the books far exceeded every expectation which had been formed, when the agreements respecting them were made: but Mr. Murray often expressed his entire satisfaction on the subject. For the Grammar, Exercises, and Key, he received seven hundred pounds; for the Abridgment, one hundred pounds; for the English Reader, three hundred and fifty pounds; for the Sequel to the English Reader, two hundred pounds; for the Introduction to the English Reader, two hundred pounds; for the Lecteur François, and the Introduction au Lecteur François, seven hundred pounds; for the Spelling-Book, and the First Book for Children, five hundred pounds; for the Selection from Horne's Commentary on the Psalms, one hundred pounds. The copyright of the Duty and Benefit of reading the Scriptures, as well as of the Power of Religion, was presented by him to the booksellers, without any pecuniary compensation. The enlargement of the Grammar in the octavo edition, and the numerous improvements in, and additions to, his other works, were always gratuitous on his part.

The demand for his grammatical works, and also for his Spelling-Book, has been so great and regular, that excepting the octavo edition of the Grammar, the types which compose them have long been kept standing. The editions which have been worked off, though numerous, have not, however, been limited to a small number of copies. For many years past, every edition of the Grammar has consisted of ten thousand copies; of the Exercises, ten thousand; of the Key, six thousand; of the Abridgment of the Grammar, twelve thousand; of the Spelling-Book, and of the First Book for Children, ten thousand. Each edition of the English Reader, and of the Introduction to the English Reader, consists of ten thousand copies; of the Sequel to the English Reader, six thousand; of the Lecteur François, and the Introduction au Lecteur François, each three thousand.—That one author should have supplied so many works on education, each of which is so extensively circulated, and so highly approved, is, I believe, unprecedented in the annals of literature. The number of editions through which Mr. Murray's grammatical and other works have passed, may be seen by referring to the list of them, at the end of this volume.

In the United States of North America, the sale of his works is rapid; and the editions are numerous. The success of his publications in his native land, afforded him much satisfaction; and was, as he observed, peculiarly grateful to his feelings.—The high approbation which his grammatical works have received, and their extensive circulation, in the United States of North America, as well as in Great Britain, is a very pleasing consideration. They will doubtless tend, in no small degree, to preserve the Anglo-American language from corruption; and to stop the progress of useless innovation. The advantages likely to accrue to both countries, from a common standard of grammatical purity and propriety, are incalculable.—The extended use of the English language is a distinguishing feature of the times in which we live: it may, perhaps, be one of the means in the hands of a wise and merciful Providence, for conveying the benefit of civilization, and the knowledge of Christianity, to the whole world.

Besides the anonymous extracts given in the preceding part of this chapter, a great number of letters to the author, from persons of high respectability in the literary world, might be produced; which contain the most favourable sentiments of his publications, and reflect great credit both on himself and on his productions. But to publish letters, however honourable to the subject of this work, without the permission of the writers, would be inconsistent with propriety, and a violation of my own principles, as well as of those of my deceased friend. They must therefore be omitted. One letter, however, from the celebrated Dr. Blair, may, very properly, be inserted in confirmation of the observations contained in this chapter, on the writings of Mr. Murray. The most material parts of it were, many years since, extracted and sent to the doctor's nephew and executer, with a request for permission to publish them. This permission was readily granted; in terms so obliging, as make it evident that no objection can arise to the publication of the whole letter. The following is an exact copy of this interesting communication; so worthy of him who paid, and of him who received, the just tribute of commendation.

Sir,

I have been honoured with your kind letter; and cannot but be very much flattered with the testimonies of esteem and regard which you are pleased to bestow: though I am humbled, at the same time, by a sense of my character's having been overrated by you, much above what it deserves. I am happy, however, that my publications have been of any service to you, in the very useful works which you have given to the public.

I return you my best thanks for the very valuable present of your works, which you have made me; and which have come safe to my hands. I have now perused a great part of them, with much pleasure and edification.—Your Grammar, with the Exercises and the Key in a separate volume, I esteem as a most excellent performance. I think it superior to any work of that nature we have yet had; and am persuaded that it is, by much, the best Grammar of the English language extant. On syntax, in particular, you have shown a wonderful degree of acuteness and precision, in ascertaining the propriety of language, and in rectifying the numberless errors which writers are apt to commit. Were I only beginning my course, as I am now (in my eighty-third year) on the point of finishing it, I should have hoped to have been much benefited, in point of accurate style, by your instructions and examples. Most useful they must certainly be to all, who are applying themselves to the arts of composition.

On your two volumes of the English Reader, I could bestow much praise for the judiciousness and propriety of the Selection, were it not that my own writings are honoured with so great a place in the work. Certainly the tendency of the whole is of the best kind; and does honour to the worthy designs and intentions of the author.—To all the friends of religion, your book on the Power of Religion on the Mind, with the apt and useful exemplifications it gives, cannot but be highly acceptable.—I am happy to find the praises of the authors of different Reviews bestowed with so much judgment and propriety as they are on your works.

As we have here not much intercourse with York, and as I have no correspondent nor acquaintance in that city, your name was unknown to me till I received the present of your books, as is also your business or profession. I should presume you are, under some character, concerned in the education of youth; and happy I must account all the young people placed under the charge of one, who not only discovers such great abilities in all that relates to English literature, but whose writings bespeak a mind fraught with the best sentiments, and the most earnest zeal for religion and virtue. *

I shall be always happy to hear of your health, success, and prosperity; and, with great regard and esteem, I am,

sir,

your most obliged,

and obedient humble servant,

Hugh Blair.

21*st. Oct.* 1800,
Edinburgh.

---

* To prevent misapprehension, I think it is necessary to observe, that Mr. Murray was, at no period of his life, engaged as a teacher of youth. Many persons, besides Dr. Blair,

The appropriate and unqualified approbation contained in the preceding letter, is the more honourable to our author, because it was bestowed by a person whose literary attainments, and professional studies, qualified him, in a peculiar manner, to judge of the works which he designates; and whose moral and religious character, as well as his years, precludes the supposition, that he did not express the genuine feelings of his mind. The merits of the works might be safely rested on the testimony which this letter contains, if there were no other recommendations of them: but their excellence is incontestably proved by the unanimous judgment of the public critics, the sentiments of

---

supposed, from the nature of his writings, that he was employed in the business of education: he even had applications on the subject; particularly from a respectable person in Holland, who, from the favourable sentiments which he had conceived of the author, on perusing his works, was desirous of placing his son under the tuition of a person so highly esteemed. From a nobleman of high rank in this country, with whom Mr. Murray was wholly unacquainted, he received an application, by letter, not indeed to educate his son, but to supply him with a tutor. Though Mr. Murray was not a teacher of youth, he entertained a high opinion of the office, and a great respect for those, who faithfully endeavour to form the young mind to knowledge and virtue. He often spoke of them, as persons engaged in one of the most important concerns of society; and whose services merit a very liberal remuneration.

many writers on education, and the almost universal admission of them into the seminaries, both of this country, and of the North American States. I sincerely hope, that they will long continue to inform and guard the minds of youth; and to serve as models of correct and chaste instruction, in various departments of science.

If any reader should think that the observations in this chapter, are too far extended, and bear the marks of undue partiality; I beg leave to state that I could scarcely have made them more limited, on an occasion in which the professed object is, to explain the nature and design, and to portray the excellences, of these publications.—I do not, however, wish to exalt the value of them above its proper level, nor to appreciate the author's literary talents more highly than they deserve. In the important business of education, I believe no person will deny that he has been eminently useful; and that his works have produced much practical good to society. And this character certainly entitles them to a respectable rank in the republic of letters. It will secure to the author, the title of the friend of youth; and the reputation of having successfully employed his time and talents, in promoting the best interests of the rising generation: a reputation which is more valuable, and dearer far, to the mind of a pious man, than the highest acquisition of mere literary fame.

The praise which Dr. Johnson bestows on Watts, may, with almost equal propriety, be applied to our author: "Whatever he took in hand was, by his incessant solicitude for souls, converted to theology. As piety predominated in his mind, it is diffused over his works. Under his direction it may be truly said, that philosophy is subservient to evangelical instruction: it is difficult to read a page without learning, or at least, wishing to be better."

THE END.

OF THE PUBLISHERS OF THE MEMOIRS

May be had the latest editions of Murray's Works, namely:

1. A First Book for Children.

The 17th edition. Price, ... *6d.*

2. An English Spelling-Book; with Reading Lessons adapted to the capacities of Children: in Three Parts. Calculated to advance the Learners by natural and easy gradations; and to teach Orthography and Pronunciation together.

The 35th edition. Price, bound, ... 1*s.* 6*d.*

3. An Abridgment of Murray's English Grammar. With an Appendix, containing Exercises in Orthography, in Parsing, in Syntax, and in Punctuation. Designed for the younger Classes of Learners.

The 92nd edition. Price, bound, ... 1*s.*

4. English Grammar, adapted to the different Classes of Learners. With an Appendix, containing Rules and Observations, for assisting the more advanced Students to write with perspicuity and accuracy.

The 40th edition. Price, bound, ... 4*s.*

5. ENGLISH EXERCISES, adapted to Murray's English Grammar: consisting of Exercises in Parsing; instances of False Orthography; violations of the Rules of Syntax; defects in Punctuation; and violations of the Rules respecting perspicuous and accurate Writing. Designed for the benefit of private Learners, as well as for the use of Schools.

The 35th edition. Price, bound, ... *2s. 6d.*

6. KEY TO THE EXERCISES, adapted to Murray's English Grammar. Calculated to enable Private Learners to become their own instructers, in Grammar and Composition.

The 17th edition. Price, bound, ... *2s. 6d.*

7. AN ENGLISH GRAMMAR: comprehending the Principles and Rules of the Language, illustrated by appropriate Exercises, and a Key to the Exercises.

In two volumes, octavo. The 5th edition, improved. Price, in boards, ... *1l. 1s.*

8. INTRODUCTION TO THE ENGLISH READER: or, A Selection of Pieces, in Prose and Poetry; calculated to improve the younger Classes of Learners in Reading; and to imbue their minds with the love of virtue. To which are added, Rules and Observations for assisting Children to read with Propriety.

The 24th edition. Price, bound, ... *3s.*

9. THE ENGLISH READER: or, Pieces in Prose and Poetry, selected from the best Writers. Designed to assist young Persons to read with propriety and effect; to improve their language and sentiments; and to inculcate some of the most important principles of piety and virtue. With a few preliminary Observations on the Principles of good Reading.

The 19th edition. Price, bound, ... 4*s.* 6*d.*

10. SEQUEL TO THE ENGLISH READER: or, Elegant Selections in Prose and Poetry. Designed to improve the highest class of learners, in reading; to establish a taste for just and accurate Composition; and to promote the interests of piety and virtue.

The 6th edition. Price, bound, ... 4*s.* 6*d.*

11. INTRODUCTION AU LECTEUR FRANÇOIS: ou, Recueil de Pièces Choisies: avec l'explication des idiotismes, et des phrases difficiles, qui s'y trouvent.

The 5th edition. Price, bound, ... 3*s.* 6*d.*

12. LECTEUR FRANÇOIS: ou, Recueil de Pièces, en Prose et en Vers, tirées des Meilleurs Écrivains. Pour servir à perfectionner les jeunes gens dans la lecture; à étendre leur connoissance de la Langue Françoise; et à leur inculquer des principes de vertu et de piété.

The 5th edition. Price, bound, ... 5*s.*

13. THE POWER OF RELIGION ON THE MIND, in Retirement, Affliction, and at the approach of Death; exemplified in the Testimonies and Experience of Persons distinguished by their greatness, learning, or virtue.

> "'Tis immortality,—'tis that alone,
> "Amidst life's pains, abasements, emptiness,
> "The soul can comfort, elevate, and fill." YOUNG.

The 18th edition. Price, bound, ... *5s.*

14. The same Work on fine paper, with a Pica letter, Octavo.

Price, in boards, ... 12*s.*

15. THE DUTY AND BENEFIT of a Daily Perusal of the HOLY SCRIPTURES, in Families.

The 2nd edition, improved. Price, ... 1*s.*

16. A SELECTION from Bishop Horne's Commentary on the Psalms.

Price, in extra boards, ... *5s.*

After a friendship of long continuance,
and now, at the age of Eighty years, I still
remain affectionately &c.

Lindley Murray.

Lithog. Fac-Simile by J. Netherclift.

APR 2 5 2000
JUN 1 5 2000

UNIVERSITY OF MICHIGAN
3 9015 04845 4477